64/15

595

THE LOVE FEAST

How Good, Natural,
Wholesome Food
Can Create
a Warm and Lasting
Christian Family Life

Graham Kerr

SIMON AND SCHUSTER
NEW YORK

1 2 3 4 5 6 7 8 9 10

Library of Congress Cataloging in Publication Data

Kerr, Graham
   The love feast.

   1. Cookery.   2. Nutrition.   3. Christian life—
1960–   I. Title.
TX652.K43   641.5′63   78–7221
ISBN 0-671-24052-8

I would like to express my thanks and my admiration to and for Ann Collier my food assistant. She is both friend and highly professional partner in the preparation of the "Take Kerr" television series and in the development of both this volume and its sister The New Seasoning.

To: Joe, Tessa, Andy, Kareena and of course Treena, who all had to suffer for my super-spiritual-destructive behavior as I tried to make my convictions legal.

G. K.

Contents

Foreword

It is usual to give the reader a few brief words on the reason why the author felt the pull to write the particular book. It is not so usual for the author's wife to do the foreword or for a wife to be brief; however, I shall endeavor to honor and respect my husband and do both.

For me, food has always been a bore! I have dieted steadily all my grown-up life, so Graham, whether he realized it or not, really wrote this book *for me* and for millions like me. To tell you I fought *gently*, cried *loudly*, thought it impossible to put into practice, would be nothing but the truth; but, because I love my Graham and my children and, incidentally, myself, I did *all* that this book has recommended. And I rejoice to say, it does work, it is worthwhile, but it is a total change and not a temporary diet.

May I offer you a word of encouragement—this book has changed our lives, which is to be expected; but to my knowledge, *The Love Feast* completely changed the food habits of five other families while still in rough manuscript form. The "horror" only takes three weeks—but what's twenty-one days to save your loved ones' lives, to feel young and vibrant again? We women are put on this earth to care for the well-being of our beloveds. Read, digest and put into practice.

Incidentally, just between you and me, the book is good reading as well as being a physical life saver. If I can do the things suggested, believe me—anyone can!

In Jesus' name,

Treena

/s/ Treena Kerr

Palm Springs,
California

Dear Reader,

This is a hard book to explain but basically it's a story about a small family that decided to be free from physiological food dependencies. You might pass it off as our move into early middle age, to an awareness of growing old, or to a desire to hop on the current natural food bandwagon.

I would prefer to think that we have all felt the need to be constantly available and effective ministers. We need our health and vitality in order to be ready to serve God the instant He decides to use us.

I am the "head" of my little family. Their physical and spiritual health and welfare are my responsibility, and I've picked up this role with an enormous sense of purpose. God gave this "little lot" into my care and I pray daily for the wisdom that might bring peace and joy to their lives. I believe God has honored these prayers and I'm privileged to share some of our life with you now.

Above all else, I want to show you the practical difference between *self-love* and *loving responsibility*, and hopefully communicate how I am dying to self and living so that my whole family may prosper in God.

In Jesus' name,

/s/ Graham Kerr

Palm Springs,
California

NOTE TO THE READER ON FOOD PRICES

As we all know too well, our grocery bills are headed for the sky!
Thus it has proved impossible constantly to update the prices of the
ingredients given in these recipes as the book moved from the stovetop
to the typewriter and through production. Please take the costs of
these recipes as a general guide only to the *relative* prices, say, of
bought sour cream versus my homemade kind, and so on throughout.

PART ONE

THE REASON

1

Free to Write

I turned the plump veal chop carefully, with tongs. It hit the safflower/sesame oil and sizzled quickly; a sharp, pleasant nutty aroma rose from the pan.

Taking a little sage, I rubbed it carefully in the palms of my hands and let it fall upon the glistening browned surface, now a touch of lemon juice, and I drained the fat. Taking a veal-stock ice cube from its plastic bag in the freezer, I slid it into the dry pan, washing the veal chop back and forth until the stock reduced to a gleaming syrup.

The broccoli had steamed to perfection, and I touched it with a brush brim-full of butter; immediately the highlights bounced back, the green deepened and glowed. The broiled tomato had just started to brown across its wide-open meaty center, and the rice was perfectly separate and fluffy in its colander high above vigorously boiling water.

It was just six in the evening and the sun was about to dip behind Castle Peak, throwing long shadows across the meadows. The ranch horses raced about, skittish at sundown.

The grass looked so dry—a bad season for rain this year in the Rockies, especially on the western slope.

"Darling," I called to Treena, "will you join me at the table?"

My wife was fasting, making her own sacrificial offering for friends—even for enemies—for healings and to thank God for answered prayers.

"Here, sit here, you can see the sunset—it's a pretty night," I observed, as I placed my simple dinner on an oval embroidered

17

placemat. A beautifully frosted glass of chilled white grape juice topped with a sprig of fresh mint stood inviting a sip.

Treena sat back from the table, her legs crossed, one foot wagging back and forth. She held a glass of water, tipping it one way, then the other. She looked at it carefully and then lifted her eyes to take in my veal chop.

The steak knife slid through the crunchy surface into a moist juicy center, the sage and lemon juice mingled with the meat juices— the aroma was just right.

Satisfied with the simplicity and elegance of the whole meal, I raised the first mouthful to my lips.

"I think you're disgusting," Treena said quietly.

The meat was already there, just enough salt, a bite from the black pepper . . . my mouth was full; I chewed and swallowed quickly.

"I beg your pardon . . . you said . . . disgusting?" My knife and fork remained poised over the chop.

"Yes—precisely." She uncrossed her legs, rose and strode across to the couch. "You pamper yourself!" The words came over her shoulder as she sat, her back to me, picking up a magazine she had already read.

Pamper! Pamper! The word jumped out at me.

"What do you mean, *pamper*? I'm only eating a simple meal that is low in calories, no fat to speak of, and it took only fifteen minutes. . . ."

The magazine hit the table with a sharp slap.

"I'll tell you what I mean!" Her green eyes were flashing.

"I'm fasting and you choose to sit there thoroughly enjoying yourself! You go fifty miles round trip to Vail and buy a milk-fed veal chop, a Rock Cornish hen, a halibut cutlet and six fresh-laid brown hen's eggs— You're obscene! Honestly, can't you see it?"

I looked down at my plate, the harmony of colors, the deep glistening green, the bright red, the crusty brown against the white fluffed rice.

"No, frankly I can't," I replied calmly. "As a matter of fact I *really* can't," I emphasized. "I told you, it's a *great* meal and I believe that one should enjoy what God provides. Now, you don't want to eat—I respect that, God blesses it but I'm not led to fast with you—so I eat; and I want to eat and enjoy . . . what's wrong with that?" Now I was the emphatic one.

Treena blew air through her nose in an explosive snort and followed it with a deep, resigned sigh. She laid her hand gently on my shoulder.

"One day you'll understand—one day; so eat up, the plate is getting cold!"

I ate, finished everything, washed up—and couldn't stop the word *pamper* from echoing about my head.

Early in the morning we set out for nearby Eagle, and as we drove in silence across the dusty sage-fringed road, the snow-clad Rocky mountains rearing high above the lower hills, I thought again of the word: pamper.

Was it true—did I really do that? Did I *still* do that?

It had been two years since I made Jesus my Lord as well as my Savior, and so much had happened, especially to my so-called gourmet image, but surely . . . not really *pampering*. Wasn't it just life, and didn't Jesus come so that we might have life and have it more abundantly?

We turned off the dirt road onto the paved surface. I reached forward to detach the four-wheel drive and settled back for the run.

The road went misty for a moment, and I realized that there were tears in my eyes.

"Lord, what's all this about?" I whispered to myself, alarmed at the feeling of self-pity.

Gluttony. You have a spirit of gluttony, God was answering through my mind, the mind that had whispered, "Lord, what's all this about?"

We took the sharp bends down into Wolcott, the valley open beneath us, the silver ribbon of the Eagle River, the little stone bridge, the corner store, the empty railroad line.

"Darling." I didn't take my eyes off the road.

"Yes, Gra?" Treena rested her hand on my arm.

"All those recipes, those countless restaurants and hotels—all the tests, research. All my life I've been so involved with food that it's become deeply ingrained in me and made me insensitive to you, when the least that you needed was to be tempted, let alone asked to join me at the table as I . . . as I . . ." Suddenly the hard-to-say words were ready to say, but I found them hard to form.

". . . as I . . . well, you said it . . . as I *pampered myself!* Immediately I spoke it out loud, the tension left me. Treena must have felt me relax. She laughed lightly and reached across with a kiss.

As the road unwound steadily, we prayed together that this unwanted echo from the past—this "pocket" of resistance to the full joy of being filled with the Holy Spirit—would leave.

I was free to move in a hitherto restricted area, free to understand it a little better, free to share that understanding when it became better understood and applied in our life.

Free to write about

The Love Feast.

2

Discovering the Substitute

A substitute is something used in place of a substance, person or feeling. Usually it is acceptable because it looks or appears to be similar to the original. Yet almost always it's second best—like vinyl and leather, polyester and cotton, margarine and butter.

Substitutes are used when the real thing is, for one reason or another, not readily available. Yet, and this is fascinating, the substitute usually brings with it some benefits that justify its acceptance. Vinyl doesn't crack like leather. Polyester is easier to wash and doesn't need ironing like cotton. Margarine is easier to spread when cold.

It's the same with the Love Substitute. It often feels and looks the same, but it isn't the original God-inspired flavor—it is basically self-imposed for selfish purposes.

As with the other substitutes, it has its worldly advantages. We feel good, we are referred to as being good; we get public acclaim and respect. People want to be our friends. In short, it's enjoyable.

A super way to illustrate the love substitute is to relate it to the home kitchen; it's one that I especially enjoy because I once majored in the art of love substitution. Then I discovered what love really meant, and I've been going through a kind of spiritual blender to find out how to apply real love in our daily lives as a family, especially in the way we eat.

Here I feel like quoting one of the most crushing comments for a Christian cook. It was Paul who made it clear to the Romans in chapter 14 that

The Kingdom of God is not food and drink but righteousness and peace and joy in the Holy Spirit.

It is this very direct piece of wisdom that got me on a new set of rails.

Paul was discussing the way in which early Christians would get quite heated about what was spiritually right to eat. Paul refers to these discussions as opinions and warns that we shouldn't gather together to dispute over opinions. Of course, the *opinions* were very current and traditional. Much had been written to guide the tribes of Israel away from dangerous food practices, and no doubt the prohibition of pork, shellfish and the mixing of dairy products with meat proved to be effective for sanitary reasons. It was also reasonable to let these common-sense laws overlap with the spiritual realm, since so much preparation of the daily food involved ritual.

When Paul said,

One believes he may eat anything, while the weak man eats only vegetables. Let not him who eats despise him who abstains, and let not him who abstains pass judgement on him who eats; for God has welcomed him.

it was truly a new deal. However, since so much legalism was involved, Paul added a safeguard.

If your brother is being injured by what you eat, you are no longer walking in love. Do not let what you eat cause the ruin of one for whom Christ died.

He goes on to say in verse 22,

The faith [to eat what you like] that you have, keep between yourself and God; happy is he who has no reason to judge himself for what he approves. But he who has doubts is condemned, if he eats, because he does not act from faith; for whatever does not proceed from faith is sin. [Phrase in brackets added.—GK]

We still have some spiritual hang-ups about food in modern times, but it isn't a key issue among Christians. I have heard few disputes about Seventh Day Adventists and their desire to be vegetarians. We respect the beliefs of those who have banned certain foods and beverages on religious grounds, even though, like Paul, we might prefer not to see these restrictions applied on a basis of belief rather than informed judgment.

But it isn't in this spiritual sense that Paul helped me. I applied his words directly to a practical problem that I had as the head of my house. How could I explain to my loved ones some of my doubts about the safety of the food we eat, without causing all kinds of legalistic mumbo jumbo to creep into our joyous, loving, free relationship?

> Do not, for the sake of food, destroy the work of God. Everything is indeed clean but it is wrong for any one to make others fall by what he eats.

It seemed that if everything was *clean,* that must mean all the artificially colored and flavored junk food on the market was approved!

But then I saw that Paul was saying that the Kingdom of God wasn't presweetened breakfast cereals and soda pop but "righteousness and peace and joy in the Holy Spirit."

All I had to do was isolate the foods now proved to be adverse to daily health, describe them accurately and give the list to my family to read, letting them first understand that these were not new laws, that there was nothing religious about the decisions to be made and that our discussions must not rupture the peace and joy that we have as a family living under the Government of God. In simple terms, nothing must stop the love from flowing.

And that was when I discovered the pendulum in my personal kitchen.

One swing takes me back over five years into the Love Substitute.

"Kareena, I've got a surprise for you!" I stuck my head out the sliding door to the garden and shouted toward the new pool area.

"Kareena!" I yelled a little louder to capture her three-year-old attention.

"Daddy's just done a super dish." That should do it. I smiled to myself.

It was 1971 and we were testing a new series of dishes for "The Galloping Gourmet." This one came from the Frogmill Inn in England's southwest and was a fairly simple layered cake smothered in almond-flavored meringue and filled with whipped cream and fresh peaches.

There was a tapping on the door. Kareena stood there slapping the palms of her hands on the glass. I slid the door back and picked her up in my arms.

"Now, darling, come and see this," I said proudly. The *gateau* was heaped high with billowing clouds of lightly browned meringue and as I cut into it, the cream filling laced with almonds and fresh peaches spilled out onto the platter.

"Ooooh, Daddy—oooh!" breathed little Kareena. Her hand flashed forward, a small pudgy finger crooked ready to scoop up a sample.

"Here, just a moment, I'll serve you," I said, and with a flourish I cut a large wedge, laid it on a plate and showed her how to eat with a cake fork.

I felt so good. Kareena gurgled with delight and wound up with cream all over her.

"Hold it!" I took a photograph—cream and all.

Now follow me as the pendulum swings over the next five years, an arc that comes out of the television world into God's Kingdom.

Kareena is now eight and we are living in the Colorado mountains.

"I've made a decision about breakfasts," I announced early one morning, before the sun had crept over the Gore Range. "We mustn't eat cardboard cornflakes. What we all need is roughage, and the best is bran. So I now want us all to take this bran cereal." I displayed the carton with another flourish, to be met by moans all around.

"Look here, Dad," said our sixteen-year-old son, Andy, "I tried that stuff and it didn't work."

"That's because you didn't give it long enough," I replied curtly.

"You see, everyone"—I tried to put a smile on it—"it's been proved now—the link between serious disorders* of the colon and a lack of adequate roughage." I could hear myself preaching, but . . . "It's for your good—I don't want to see any of you dying that way."

The family just sat there glumly, resisting without adding further comment.

"Well, that's settled, then." I opened the packet and passed it round.

"One ounce each, please," I instructed as they shook the gray-

---

* Such as diverticulosis.

brown squirts of compacted bran into their bowls, adding 2 percent low-fat milk.

The meal went by in silent hostility.

In the first scene, the dessert was a nutritional disaster, and my enjoyment was in giving it to our precious three-year-old, thereby developing a reaction in her that "love from Daddy equals a slice of creamy sweet cake." Just five years later, the same "love from Daddy" equaled one ounce of bran cereal.

The early *worldly* love felt good, but my new brand of Kingdom love wasn't half so satisfactory; yet I could fall back on the promises the report held that my little family would not die of cancer of the colon.

The pendulum had swung full course. In fact, it had really broken through the side of the grandfather clock!

True love, God's love, always provides an element of freedom of choice for those old enough to express an opinion. In the first case I had exercised my desire upon Kareena. I *knew* she'd love the cake and that she'd love me for serving it to her—even if I hadn't seen her in weeks because of the incredible schedule we kept. In the second case I had imposed my will again, but this time I'd been loving them all, I'd been available and it was selfless love because I *knew* they'd hate the bran cereal.

Both had been imposed for my selfish reason, so both were not in keeping with Paul's admonition: "The Kingdom of God is not a Frogmill Meringue *Gateau* or bran cereal—it's righteousness and peace and joy in the Holy Spirit."

There it was, written almost two thousand years ago. You could paddle in a sea of lecithin, honey and seaweed or stumble over acres of hotdogs and ice cream; it didn't matter if the Love Factor had been replaced by *self-imposed love*!

Now I was going to explore the totally unknown country of "freedom to choose for a young, energetic, healthy, loving family."

How could this be done?

3

How Do We Choose?

First, you and I need to agree that all this is necessary and that there may be a need in your household to think about the way you and your family are eating.

Bad nutrition starts out as something *done to us*; it continues as something we *do to ourselves*. This means that the way we eat, as adults, is largely environmental—it's a composite of the way we were fed as children.

Among the present generation, this tradition is rapidly disintegrating with the advances being made daily by the fast-food industry—very few of whose members pretend to serve foods warmly suggestive of home and comfort and "motherhood and apple pie."

Some statistics go as far as to assert that out of twenty-one meal opportunities per week, we take as few as seven meals in our own homes. From this we can simply deduce that the nation's nutrition has left the parents' hands and has been delivered to massive corporations.

Our son, Andy, recently graduated, and within one week he began a summer job in the desert close to Palm Springs, as a "dry-waller," hanging sheetrock in partially completed frame houses. It is hot, dry work in temperatures that easily top 115°.

Treena and I discussed the lunch problem. We could release him to finger-lickin', build your own billion-a-year businesses, or we could continue the school lunch routine but beefed up to provide for his real needs.

There was no discussion. Our love for Andy easily topped any inconvenience. A large black plastic lunch pail was purchased and a one-gallon insulated water dispenser. Into this went the best food that we could find, not "weirdo" food, but things he liked to eat, full of protein, on whole-grain buttered bread.

The temptation to collapse into compromise continued, of course. When your fellow workers have been conditioned to eat "motel pillow" hamburger rolls and drink soda pop, it's hard to arrive on a rough building site with whole-wheat bread and fruit juice!

The first phase of disintegration was to move into the bread-roll area, then into a high-glucose fruit drink for energy. We saw this as a mistake as soon as our Love Factor returned to its proper place. We had made the classic error of being sympathetic about peer pressure. We had actually helped him succumb to pressure in a delicate area where his health was literally in the balance; clearly a Love Substitute decision.

Does it all start with food dependencies? Is this where the first compromises take place on the tedious road of cigarettes, beer, liquor, soft and hard drugs? Could it really begin, for some young people, at the "Dream Whip Ice Cream Parlor" because of parental apathy?

The whole wheat is now back, the principle is understood by us all and the bulk of the liquid he takes is water. The flavored drinks are a constantly changing experiment that rule out most of the sugar and all of the artificial sweeteners, colorings or flavorings.

The working lunch boosted Andy's "at home" meals by five a week, and we have recovered control of his nutritional intake. Best of all, Andy feels good about its being *his* decision and *his* choice for *his* health.

This is just an example of the sneaky way that the archenemy, compromise, erodes our best intentions. But what of the overview, the whole domestic food picture?

As of this date we see the major issues grouped as follows.

Sugar and sugar substitutes, simple carbohydrates
Fat and oils
Salt and monosodium glutamate (MSG)
Restructured foods
Artificial colors and flavors
Chemical preservatives
Nutrification—enrichment with added nutrients.

In order to effectively choose between sugared, colored "kiddie" cereals and bran we simply must know what we are getting into and not merely respond to the ninety-second news item on television or radio.

I enjoy the writings about Solomon, especially in chapter 4 of the first book of Kings. Here was a man to whom God had given "wisdom and understanding beyond measure," and one of the side effects of this provision was that he had "peace on all sides" and "every man was under his vine and under his fig tree."

That's such a peaceful vision—in the heat of the day, a man in white robes just sitting in the shade of a bountiful fruit tree! And doing so because he wasn't threatened, at peace because his king was wise.

So it is with us in our own homes. We too should have peace. But we don't, because our "king," the government, is caught in a compromise between vested interest in chemical engineering for the sake of financial growth and on the other hand an appalling lack of knowledge in nutritional science.

Should we go to the wave of books on nutrition that preach the latest best guess about everything from warts to wedding nights as being subject to the all-powerful super n for nutrition? No! I feel we need to read in order to learn, but our real source is our Creator—God our Father, the one who made us and loves us.

But how do we receive his advice?

We read and rationalize with the brains and intellect he gave us; then, armed with all the known facts, we ask Father to help us to choose.

Leaving Father out of the issue simply puts us back into the worldly confusion that exists and can also lead us up some strange paths.

For example, I know that niacin (vitamin B_3) has been used to treat cases of schizophrenia. But I also know that one or two types of schizophrenia are in fact made worse by this selfsame vitamin: result, worldly confusion. But I also know that God, through the working of his Holy Spirit, also heals schizophrenia and never, ever worsens such a problem! Therefore I reason that my trust must be in God; he is my Father and he loves me. That makes me feel I'm sheltered by the vine.

So I go like Solomon to Father and I say to him,

Give thy servant therefore an understanding mind to govern thy people, that I may discern between good and evil.

God was pleased with this request and replied to Solomon, in chapter 3 of the first book of Kings,

Because you have asked this, and have not asked for yourself long life or riches or the life of your enemies, but have asked for yourself understanding to discern what is right, behold, I now do according to your word. Behold, I give you a wise and discerning mind. . . .

So I feel confident that I might ask Father for such a mind for my family, to sift the facts of the world and to decide what our family should eat. In this way I can come to terms with my fellow man, who could charge me with superspirituality without knowledge, and I might respond to my God as the source of my supply rather than lean on my own understanding.

Therefore, I've done my homework and provided for you the worldly facts (as presented to us all by the best that science can offer), and I encourage you to pray to Father for his help to choose what is beneficial for your family.

But *please* don't make these decisions religious, because your choice will then be made into a rule; and rules become law, and law gradually eliminates love.

4

Eliminate the Negative!

Books lay heaped on my desk, dozens of sheets of legal-size paper covered with fine small notes—my reading glasses splayed out too far to fit my ears.

It was the final piece of research. The work was done on sugar, fat, sodium, artificial colors, flavors, engineered foods, and I was coming to the end of preservatives when I hit nitrites and nitrates. Beatrice Trum Hunter, in her excellent little *Fact Book on Food Additives and Your Health* (Keats, 1972), gives a typically uncolored factual appraisal that is chilling enough:

> Although experts testified [at the Congressional Hearings on Regulations of Food Additives and Medicated Animal Feeds, March 1971] that nitrites at current high levels, used mainly for "cosmetic purposes" [to improve and keep color], are hazardous, government officials saw "no immediate hazard."

The government has been presented with evidence that these chemicals are believed responsible for cases of severe arthritic symptoms and reduction of ability to store vitamin A in the liver. There is evidence of permanent epilepsy-like changes in brain activity with doses only slightly larger than might be expected from a frequent consumption of cured meats and sausages, including frankfurters.

But by far the most upsetting statement came from Doctors Epstein and Lijinsky of the University of Nebraska, who stated that on the basis of "significant studies," they had had to conclude that nitrates may be carcinogenic, mutagenic *and* teratogenic as well as toxic!

Now, let me admit to you that I didn't have a clue to what most of that meant, so I looked it up.

SODIUM NITRATES, NITRITES: Chemical compounds used as preservatives and "color fixatives" in cured meat, meat products and cured fish (also called saltpeter).

CURED MEATS, FISH: Meats and fish treated to a "salting" or "brine pickled" process such as bacon, bologna, frankfurters, corned beef, deviled ham, meat spreads, boned meats, spiced ham, uncooked smoked ham, smoked cured shad or salmon and tuna.

DECLARATION: The label on all these products must display the use of the chemicals by using the name nitrites or nitrates as the case may be.

CARCINOGEN: Any substance that produces cancer.

MUTAGEN: Any agent or substance, such as X-rays, mustard gas, etc., capable of noticeably increasing the frequency of mutation (a sudden variation in some inheritable characteristic in a germ cell of an animal or plant, as distinguished from a variation resulting from generations of gradual change). In other words, a genetic disturbance!

TERATOGEN: An agent, such as a chemical, disease, etc., that causes malformation of a fetus (the offspring in the womb from the end of the third month of pregnancy until birth; prior to that it is called an embryo).

These doctors were saying, in our terms, that as a result of their scientific studies they felt it proper to alert our government to the fact that the use of these kinds of preservative salts in our meat products was, in their opinion, capable of producing:

CANCER
GENETIC DISTURBANCE
MALFORMATION OF UNBORN CHILDREN

Our government responds to this and many other studies with the phrase "No immediate hazard"!

I went on with my research.* It was almost four o'clock in the

---

* Authorities consulted include: Dale Hattis, Stanford School of Medicine; Dr. Jacobson, Massachusetts Institute of Technology; University of California Medical Center, San Francisco. The following books in particular proved helpful: Jacqueline Verrett and Jean Carper, *Eating May Be Hazardous to Your Health* (Simon and Schuster, 1974), and Ethel H. Renwick, *Let's Try Real Food* (Kentwood, MI: Zondervan, 1976).

afternoon, and nowhere had I read anything *good* about nitrites. The government had imposed more stringent restrictions on their use in foods such as bacon, but the reason had to do with color rather than preservation, and far less harmful chemicals could be used in their place.

Big business, it would seem, has a good deal to do with how Washington ticks.

I sat there just staring at the papers, considering the families hurt by the effects of chemical warfare waged on us by business interests. I had been part of that scene as a highly paid consultant and promoter. I had sat on taste panels and given my expert judgment about salt, sugar and fat levels designed to bring the customer back to our product. We were in the business of manufacturing a *dependency*, of "hooking" a customer.

So we get pretty pink bacon; so we also take the risk of getting cancer or of sustaining genetic damage or the horror of malformation which could seriously affect our children's lives even before they are brought into the world.

I had asked God for wisdom for my family. He gave it, but along with wisdom comes responsibility. I could see that I wasn't equipped as a scientist to deal with the issue. Just reading isn't enough to *prove* a technical issue and impose a ban where hitherto business had won.

Then I saw that it wasn't necessary for me and for this book. I have been called to serve my family, and in passing on our "life" to your family, I am totally discharging my responsibility. I had been moved to tears for those so cruelly hurt, but I was no longer ignorant, so I resolved to start where I lived.

I put all the papers neatly together and set out for my daily walk/run exercise, an hour of mixed discipline. I flopped into a kitchen chair on my return and was talking with Treena as she made Andy's "superlunch" for the next day.

On the bench was a neat stack of sliced bologna. I knew the promise I'd made about not preaching, but the "facts" were still hot in my heart.

"Now, that will . . ." My preaching finger had raised itself and was wagging at the limp slice of bologna in Treena's hand.

"What—you mean I can't use this either?" Her eyes filled instantly with tears.

"How am I going to feed him—I've got nothing left—look." She gestured with the bologna slice at the open fridge.

"There's nothing there!"

"You and your preaching!" She dealt the bologna like cards across the floor.

"You might as well throw out this and this and this." She pulled out tins from the pantry. "They've all got your nitrates or whatever they are." Her fists were clenched tightly by her side as Andy came in. The bologna was all over the floor.

"What's up?" he asked quietly.

"Your father is what's up." Treena poked a knife in my direction.

"What I did, Andy," I explained in a very quiet voice, "was bring some of my research to your mother's attention, specifically about nitrosamines that are possibly synthesized in the digestive tract by the residual nitrite ions and secondary amines." It was wordy, but I didn't know how else to explain it.

"What's more," Treena added with heavy emphasis, "these tins have to be thrown out *too!*" She handed Andy some corned beef to throw out. Andy looked at the price on the can and in disgust threw it into the garbage.

"I don't get you guys!" he huffed, and left the kitchen abruptly.

I sat there, inspecting my shoe closely as Treena continued to explain her reaction.

"Your timing is, as usual, incredible." She was slicing cheese to replace the bologna.

"How else could I have reacted?" I interrupted. "Today I read about a really harmful additive and came in to see you using the very meat in Andy's sandwiches. Do I have to wait for an appropriate moment to save his life?" I felt so totally *right* that I began to be a little uncertain.

"Let me explain, Mr. Super-Religious-Scientist." Treena was much calmer. "You could have seen me using it and gone out to the store, bought some nonnitrate protein and given it to me saying, "I bought this to replace the bologna in Andy's sandwiches.""

I smiled suddenly. What a super idea; then it would have been a loving gesture all around!

"I'm sorry, kitten—please forgive me." I stood up and held her shoulder gently.

"Oh that's all right—I do forgive you, and really, I understand your concern." She smiled.

The battle was over, but once again I'd had my warning. I had researched over fifty adverse foods and had managed to foul the whole Love Factor with just one emergency issue without thinking.

From that moment I stilled my tongue and sat down to write out, in much less scientifically wordy terms, an appraisal of the negatives for my family to discuss, to help us decide how to go about dealing with them in our daily food.

5

The Sugar Decision

In this chapter I give you exactly the same decision opportunities I gave to my family. We discussed these at our family-night meeting (every Thursday) and reached our own conclusions.

Sugar is burned by your body cells to generate the energy necessary to run the cell. In a sense this is like a car battery: you can put a massive charge into a low battery and get it up enough to work, but there is a danger of buckling the plates. A better way is to put it on trickle-charge overnight, but clearly better still is to have the alternator put the charge back into the battery as you drive.

So it is with sugar. We must have glucose in our blood. It's called blood sugar, and if it gets too high or too low, we react by getting sick.

The most efficient sugar is the kind that is constantly being added to the blood through a kind of alternator. Many of our daily foods are converted into glucose in our bodies without actually tasting sweet in the first place. Foods like potatoes, rice and milk are good examples of *surprise sugar*.

The *no-surprise sugars* come as sucrose or refined sugar made from cane, beets, or corn. This is called simple because that's just the way it looks under a microscope. Only two molecules group to form the complete sugar.

Because they are so simple, they go readily into the bloodstream. We get too much, all at once. It's like putting your foot on the gas before starting an engine—you literally flood the system.

One of the effects we can get is to brutalize the Islets of Langerhans (a rather exotic travel-brochure description of a section

D-Glucose + D-Fructose = Sucrose

of a gland called the pancreas that releases insulin). The constant flooding of this gland can upset its operation and cause an insulin-supply problem (one element of diabetes).

Another problem is the "roller-coaster syndrome" of blood sugar. The exciting slow smooth ride up to the top of a huge roller coaster is wonderful but the sudden steep drop is the inescapable aftermath. So it is with the "candy popper." The simple-carbohydrate sugar gets directly into the bloodstream instantly causing a smooth "up," or high feeling; but it doesn't last—the need for another "shot" comes quickly and with increasing frequency as the pleasure-responding system reacts to the stimulus.

Now take away the instant no-surprise sugar and you are left with one or more of the following reactions. Just tick them off if they *feel* like you.

Nervous	Heart palpitations
Exhausted	Phobias or fears
Irritable	Nightmares
Dizzy	Nervous breakdown
Chronic worrying	Mental confusion
Tremor	Crying spells
Depression	Muscle cramps
Forgetfulness	Numbness
Poor digestion	Uncoordination
Trembling inside	Tingling of lips
Headaches	Suicidal feelings
Drowsiness	Lack of concentration
Wakefulness	Indecisiveness
Unprovoked anxiety	Unusual behavior

Noises in ears	Gasping for breath
Allergies	Yawning, sighing
Blurred vision	Itching and crawling skin

By no means should you think that you are sick if you have multiple reactions akin to the above, but you may certainly assume that you are not in good abounding health. It is *possible* that you may have eaten so many simple no-surprise sugars that your system has become hypoglycemic, which means the blood-sugar level falls rapidly like the roller coaster and you feel lousy.

Notice please, that most of the symptoms are concerned with the thought process. Thought is a brain function. All tissues except the brain may derive energy from protein or fat, but the brain is almost totally dependent upon blood sugar for food because it cannot absorb and use oxygen without the presence of sugar. This lack of blood sugar produces the down-type thought processes.

Let me give you another list:

Love	Kindness
Joy	Faithfulness
Peace	Gentleness
Patience	Self-control

These too are thought patterns, but they are radiant patterns: they can be seen to exist, because all of them affect people who are in their company.

Now, if, as a result of our brain's being "starved," we have down thoughts rather than radiant thoughts, we have to assume that an opposite force might be attempting to jam our outgoing system. In this case the tool used to scramble our better instincts is sugar!

The consumption of sugar in the United States and Great Britain falls approximately between 104 and 170 pounds per person per year. These figures mean consuming ⅓ teaspoon each 30 minutes, 24 hours a day, 7 days a week! How can this possibly be accurate?

I discovered that we receive vast quantities indirectly through the *hidden sugar* supplied by the food-manufacturing industry that now exceeds seven million tons each year. To give you some idea of how the simple sugars get out of the teaspoon and into our food, the American Dental Association produced the list shown in Table 1.

TABLE 1

CANDY

	Tsps. of sugar
Chocolate bar, 1 average size	7
Chocolate fudge, 1½" square	4
Chocolate mint, 1 med. (20/lb.)	3
Chewing gum, 1 stick	½
Marshmallow, 1 large	1½

CAKE

Chocolate, 1/12 cake (2 layer iced)	15
Angel food, 1/12 cake (large cake)	6
Sponge 1/10 (average size)	6
Cream puff (eclair) custard filled (iced)	5
Dougnut, 3" dia. plain	4
Brownie, 2 x 2¾"	3

ICE CREAM

Sherbet, ½ cup	5–6
Ice cream, ½ cup	5–6

PIE

Cherry pie, ⅙ med. pie	14
Raisin pie, ⅙ med. pie	13
Apple pie, ⅙ med. pie	12
Pumpkin pie, ⅙ med. pie	10

DRINKS

Sweet-flavored soda, 6 oz.	4⅓
Chocolate milk, 1 cup (5 oz. milk)	6
Eggnog, 1 glass (8 oz. milk)	4½
Cocoa, 1 cup (5 oz. milk)	4

SPREADS/SAUCES

Chocolate Sauce, 1 tbsp.	4½
Jams, 1 level tbsp.	3
Marmalade, 1 level tbsp.	3
Jelly and syrups, 1 level tbsp.	2½

FRUITS

Rhubarb, stewed, sweetened, ½ cup	8
Prunes, stewed, sweetened* (4–5 med)	8
Fruit cocktail, ½ cup	5
Peaches, pears, canned in syrup,* 2 halves	3½

* Plus ½ tbsp. juice.

BREAKFAST CEREALS

> Since the range is so complex, we must look at the
> average of about 40% of the contents consisting of
> simple sugar.

A look at one natural food fiber cereal could be of interest. Of the total weight of a 1-ounce dry serving (21 grams), we find that 14 grams are starch and 7 grams are sugars. By weight, 33⅓ percent sugar in a natural food product!

The cereal industy explains that "sugar helps children eat their vitamins." But please note that the cereal has to be "enriched" with the vitamins!

Dr. John Yudkin, a famous British nutritional scientist, has said that sugar:

> Hardens arteries
> Attacks the heart (increases triglycerides)
> Leads to
>> Bad eyesight
>> Unhealthy skin
>> Tooth decay
>> Indigestion
>> Ulcers

He goes on to say,

> If a fraction of what is already known about the effects of
> sugar were to be revealed as pertaining to any other material
> used as a food additive, the material would be promptly
> banned.*

He gives details of a study conducted on St. Helena, where the people consume far less fat than we do, smoke less, get lots of exercise but have a high rate of coronary deaths. The *only* unusual diet factor is their high sugar consumption!

Dr. Jean Mayer, the Harvard nutritionist, adds an interesting note: "Both the decay-producing cariogenic [decay of teeth] and

---

* *Sweet and Dangerous* (New York: Bantam Books, 1972).

caloric impact of sugar—white, raw, or brown—are equally devastating."

So what can we do in this addicted situation?

We know we need glucose, or blood sugar. We know we need that it be provided gradually. We know that simple carbohydrates enter immediately. We know that complex carbohydrates take time. Therefore we could look at complex carbohydrates as a source of supply for our blood-sugar needs rather than the straight goods!

Complex carbohydrates are found in grain, vegetables and fruits: the fresh, natural nonprocessed foods in the marketplace. Simple carbohydrates represent the refining process in products such as table sugar, white flour, polished rice, sweetened and unsweetened bakery goods made from white refined flour, many precooked breakfast cereals and *all* highly sweetened desserts, beverages, candies and ice creams.

And so we come to that old familiar cry: "But what's left?"

First, the sweet replacements for those who are not overweight and do not have hypoglycemia.

Raisins
Dates
Figs
Prunes
Grapes
Prune juice

Molasses, honey or *any* syrups are not complex carbohydrates and should be used sparingly in place of sugar.

Sweet replacements for the overweight and hypoglycemics.

Fresh fruits and fresh fruit juices
Sweet potatoes and yams

Such dishes as milk puddings can be sweetened with milk's natural lactose sugar in combination with the complex carbohydrates of dried and/or fresh fruits (see pages 234 and 235 for recipes). Although I suggest some caution here due to a growing awareness that milk products containing lactose may not be tolerated by certain individuals. If you or one of your family experiences dyspepsia, then please check it out with your doctor, who can prescribe a simple, inexpensive lactose tolerance test.

To follow the idea of cutting back on sugar genuinely, we will have to consider the way we use or receive sugar.

In tea, coffee or milk drinks
In pies, cakes and cookies
In all packaged gelatin desserts
In all regular ice cream products
In all sweetened beverages
In all precooked products that have sugar on the label in the first three named ingredients. This includes all cereals.

When we consider, we are really asking God to direct us, or convince us. If we feel genuinely moved to action, then I believe—since the result can only be beneficial—that such prompting is the clear work of the Spirit and that you ought to say, "Father, I'll offer no resistance—please clear the way for me to make the changes."

I would then expect either an immediate or a gradual elimination of both obvious and hidden sugar supplies. God doesn't impose hardship but rewards willingness by making what would have been our suffering into an easy, exciting and fulfilling undertaking. Remember, your body is his temple, and he obviously would prefer to have it thoroughly cleansed; but more than that, he would like to see it kept clean and not have to face on-and-off annual spring cleanings!

Here is one way of making an inspired reduction. We have broken the total change into three phases. You simply undertake Phase One until life is normal and your family stops talking about it in sacrificial terms. Then go on to Phase Two and finally, when Phase Three is reached, you've made a complete transition.

This proposal is geared for those who are not convinced by what you may have read. They may love and respect you as the home cook, but they have also grown to respond to sweet things in an agreeable way. If you decide to totally eliminate sugar on an apparent impulse, it will be hard for them to reconcile your action with the giving love we all agree should be the starting point of this whole exercise.

Therefore, while you may agree with your mate to exclude sugar totally and ask Father to help you to undertake such a massive change, you might at the same time let the children know that you appreciate them and want it not to hurt.

The good thing about sugar reform is, the lower the intake, the lower the craving; so the gradual reduction for the unconvinced will eventually convince because the desire will go and with it the sweet-tooth reaction. Almost everyone who has severely reduced sugar will tell you that the old familiar sweet things of last month taste sickening to the newly reconditioned taste buds.

So now, here is the "Phase Out" system for the unconvinced.

PHASE ONE

Where *sugar* is taken in tea or coffee, the quantity should be reduced by half.

Where *artificial sweetner* is used, eliminate altogether and replace with 1 level teaspoonful of sugar.

In all *desserts* that call for sugar, reduce sugar by ⅓ and add 1 teaspoon fresh lemon juice to replace each 1 tablespoon of sugar eliminated.

Add club soda to *sweetened flavored sodas*. This will mean that direct consumption from can or bottle will be ended. We suggest that you start with 25% soda and stop when they notice! (This is a tough one to keep going. You may need to discuss its value with the family, even conduct a taste test in which you add 10%–20%–30% soda and ask which they prefer. Each 10% will equal approximately ½ teaspoon sugar.)

Reduce *candy* purchases gradually. Start out by not giving candy as a prize for being good. The nearly $4 billion we spend on our tooth decay could be at least halved by cutting out the "there's a good little boy/girl" gift.

Convert to natural *ice cream* from stores that stock whole foods. It is made from cream and honey and contains none of the additives that the major grocery chains merchandise. We did this and found we need much less (which is great because it costs much more!).

Eliminate all chocolate-coated and/or cream-filled *cookies*. Keep them plain non-sugar-encrusted.

Bake *cakes* with reduced sugar; don't buy them from a store.

Cut out *jams* and *jellies* and replace them with honey. If you meet resistance, try our no-cook jam recipe on page 243.

PHASE TWO

Cut sugar down to ½ teaspoon in tea or coffee (iced or hot).

Reduce sugar content in desserts by 50%. Where they no longer work—even with the lemon-juice substitute—simply remove them from your menu, and rely more upon fresh fruit and cheese (see Desserts, page 225).

Begin to serve fresh fruit juices with club soda to add the desired "prickly" mouth-feel. Serve as replacement for Cokes, 7-Up and other sweetened beverages. You can make these yourself or buy them prepared at juice bars, where they tend to be too expensive. Try this twice per week only.

Take out all candy bowls or boxes of chocolates, and all visible supplies of sugared foods. Do not supply candy in lunch boxes but include carob-coated protein bars; try these out until you find the one best liked.

Reduce cookie baking at home to zero. Buy only small arrowroot biscuits. Don't be tempted by whole-grain supernutritious cookies —they can be deadly to the weight!

Do not bake any more cakes—only whole-grain breads (see our chapter on superbreads, page 187).

Cut out all *sugar-added* cereals—allow children to add honey for sweetness—but don't overdo it. Honey is a simple carbohydrate.

Use raisins, dates, or dried figs to sweeten foods.

PHASE THREE

Cut out all *sugar* and sugar substitutes in tea or coffee (iced or hot).

Eliminate all *desserts* that need added sugar. Replace sugar with dates, raisins, figs or honey (in very small quantities).

Remove all *carbonated sweetened or artificially sweetened soft drinks*. Replace with unsweetened fruit juices, preferably made in your own home.

Decide to buy no more *candy* for any purpose including birthdays or Christmas. There is no celebration that is suited to candy and what it does to the human system, other than perhaps funerals.

Cut out all cookie and baked-goods purchases and replace with a bowl of sunflower seeds, adding a few raisins to the bowl for sweeteners. Carrot sticks are also sweet and make good snack food where once only the cookie would have done the job!

Buy no prepared food that lists sugar as an ingredient.

When this is done you are off the sugar hook, and you can be quite sure that your obedience as a family will result in much better health.

We need to add one word about eating out, either at friends' homes or in restaurants.

An occasional transgression is not a problem. We can be certain that this is so, because an occasional dessert will taste sickeningly sweet. It is only when the soft drink or candy or pie tastes *great* that you know that you are still physically on the hook and need to drop that spoon as though it were red hot.

At a friend's house, it is better to draw your hostess to one side before a meal and tell her about your sugar reform. Then she'll be prepared for you. The problem with a friend arises only when you nibble and don't eat; that can be misconstrued as a dislike for her cooking!

6

The Fat Decision

I'm going to admit right up front that as a result of literally years of study and questioning I'm no better off than when I started on this matter.

I do know that fat in excess is a killer; everyone agrees to that. But then, a man in Maryland recently died from an excessive consumption of carrot juice!

The real question is: How much is excessive? The answer largely depends upon which camp you belong to. Are you a polyunsaturate, cholesterol believer or do you see no direct connection and consume dairy products with some restrictions?

Since experts hotly disagree, I have no desire or ability to attempt a brilliant *coup de grâce*. I'm going to join Carlton Fredericks and suggest that where experts disagree, you should take a safe path.

Experts at the Longevity Center in Santa Barbara have proved to my satisfaction that severe cases of cardiovascular diseases can be reversed by heavily reduced fat intake (10 percent of a day's total intake) with correspondingly low protein (10 percent), leaving 80 percent to be found from only complex carbohydrates.

However, I'm not so sure that a person who does not show high coronary-risk factors will necessarily be blessed by such a diet. To be sure, the Longevity Center does go up to 15 percent fat in less severe cases, but that is still an uncommonly difficult regimen to keep.

During World War II, the British population were treated to a sharp fat reduction, down to 33 percent. This caused numerous complaints that were specific enough to be noticed among the natural level of complaints found in my homeland. After the rationing period ended, fat consumption returned to 38–40 percent and the complaints vanished.

Somewhere between 15 percent and 38 percent lies an answer, but it isn't hard and fast, and each individual appears to have markedly differing needs. I suspect that if we were simply to accept that fat isn't fabulous, we would be able to restrict our intake to the 25–35 percent level without too much of a problem. We need, however, to list some fat sources and fat uses that must be established as excessive.

Cream. The frequent addition of cream to sauces and soups will unquestionably improve the appeal of the dish, but it is a heavy fat onslaught. Nonfat dry milk powder with a little corn starch or arrowroot mixed to a light paste with water will do a less offensive job.

Whipped cream. Desserts piled high are a major threat. No more than 1 tablespoon should be taken with a dessert (see also our low-fat whipped cream, page 231).

Butter. "Fine" recipes call for a "nut of butter" (meaning a walnut, *shell on*). This is thoroughly addictive, as the sauce or casserole is probably already loaded with fat. It is better to add 1 tablespoon of 8 percent sodium soy sauce as a substitute.

Steaks. The high cost of steaks will tempt you to leave the ("choice" grade) fat intact, especially on the barbecue grill. All visible fat should be cut off to remove excess; there is already ample fat marbled into the lean meat.

Hamburgers. Regular hamburger is well in excess of healthful low fat levels. It is better to buy a meat grinder (it doesn't *have* to be an electric one) and put very lean meat through it when needed.

Buttering. Vegetables look great when spotted with chunks of butter, but it's one of our most serious fat excesses. Frankly—and I do recognize exactly what this is going to mean—I would recommend that you stop buttering vegetables immediately, especially those baked or boiled potatoes.

Shortening and margarines. Some of the most highly controversial fats can be found in vegetable- and/or coconut-oil products that have been hydrogenated, or treated in such a way as to convert a perfectly natural (oil) molecule into an absolutely unnatural stiffened molecule. Until more is known about the effects of this basic tinkering with nature, it would be well to avoid all products labeled "hydrogenated vegetable oils." This includes all peanut butters unless the label specifies otherwise.

Eggs. Here are centered some of the most heated debates. The egg is used as a measure for protein, so nearly perfect is it as a source. But the egg also contains the greatest concentration of cholesterol—but then again it also holds a massive dose of lecithin, which is recognized as one of the most effective means of reducing cholesterol. So, if I take an egg I get excellent, low-cost protein but I also take on cholesterol—but I also get lecithin, which should compensate!

We no longer eat eggs for breakfast. Our needs are fulfilled with 4 oz. *fresh* orange juice, 1 oz. mixed whole-grain cereal, 2 oz. nonfat certified raw milk, a tablespoon of low-fat plain yogurt and some black raspberries or a banana. We have one slice of whole-grain bread with butter and honey, and that does the trick for me. Andy, who works harder than almost anyone else I know, starts the day on:

> 6 *oz. nonfat certified raw milk*
> 1 *banana*
> 1 *tbsp. honey*
> 1 *tbsp. lecithin*
> 1 *tbsp. brewer's yeast*
> 1 *whole egg*

This is blended, tightly covered and left in the refrigerator overnight. Thus Andy gets an egg a day, and we consume fewer than six a week in the form of an omelet or in some other dishes. I'm not saying this is *right*; I'm only illustrating that it works without any feeling of loss or rebellion.

Following these recommendations should bring down your fat consumption from a U.S. average about 40–50 percent (which is dangerous), to roughly 25–30 percent, which should be a positive yet normal adjustment for the average low-risk C.A.D.

C.A.D. is short for *coronary heart disease,* which in turn means *failure of the arteries to allow a free flow of blood.*

C.A.D. has been investigated in many studies costing millions of dollars, but the one most widely respected and frequently quoted is that made in Framingham, Massachusetts, which began in 1948 and involved 2336 men and 2873 women aged 29–62 years. During a twenty-year period it was discovered that the group could be divided into three major sectors:

1. Those who could be expected to have C.A.D. = high risk
2. Those who might not be so vulnerable to C.A.D. = low risk
3. Those who were especially subject to C.A.D. = special risk

The high risks are computed as follows:

Low serum cholesterol
Normal blood pressure } = ⅓ standard risk of
Nonsmokers   C.A.D. = low risk

BUT IF

High serum cholesterol
High blood pressure } = 10 times the standard risk
Smoker   of C.A.D. = high risk

AND IF

Relatives have had C.A.D.
Also suffers from hypertension, diabetes
  mellitus, gout or xanthomatosis   } = SPECIAL RISK
40–50 years old, businessman with driving
  ambition and heavy smoker

We can now add to this study another important scientific observation concluded in 1976 in Tecumseh, Michigan, where researchers have found some evidence to link obesity with cholesterol and triglyceride levels. This would add obesity to the high-risk and special-risk factors. Yet it has been noted in a study evaluating San Francisco longshoremen that obese men taking vigorous exercise had fewer C.A.D. symptoms than the normally obese sedentary person.

Let's look at the picture again:

High- or special-risk elements are in order of priority:
1. Relatives who have had C.A.D.
2. 40–50 years, male, driving ambition and heavy smoker
3. Smoker

4. High serum cholesterol
5. Also suffers from: Hypertension
                            Diabetes mellitus
                            Gout
                            Xanthomatosis
6. Sedentary work with little exercise
7. High blood pressure
8. Overweight

If in any way this looks like you, or one of your family or one of your friends, then I would suggest that you cut down on sugar, fat and salt immediately.

7

The Salt Decision

If you are skipping pages, I would urge you to return to pages 35–49 and read through with me about the Sugar Decision and the Fat Decision. Both sections contain comments that apply equally to the problem of salt.

Our taste sensation is limited to receiving sweet, sour, salt, bitter and something called "piquant." We have dealt with sweet and the mouth-feel of fat: now it's time for salt.

If we prepare, cook and eat a varied and adequate supply of fresh vegetables, we will receive sufficient salt for our normal body needs. There is no physiological need to add salt!

That's step one in the argument—let's see where we get bogged down.

We are a people preconditioned to receive salted foods, especially in the snack sector, where we are known to respond well to either sweet or salt. In an effort to make money, for which one can surely blame anyone living in our Western culture, the manufacturer, seeking repeat customers, will add either salt or sugar or both until the saturation point is reached.

Now, I'm not being some kind of lofty do-gooder in saying this. I have often participated in taste panels for huge companies, to determine (as an expert) just what it would take to bring customers back for a second purchase and thereafter make them lifelong customers. Where "the rubber met the road" was the *hookability* of the sugar or salt content, and this meant going up to the maximum my taste would tolerate.

Both salt and sugar are "safe"; they aren't looked upon by people as chemicals because they stand on the ordinary kitchen shelf. They are also inexpensive and react in predictable ways.

So what is wrong with using them?

They both create dependencies!

Salt is added to low-cost foods, usually carbohydrates, to spark their otherwise bland taste. This then adds an unnatural dimension to a food that has a fairly low appeal and causes us to return to it, not for the bland basic unit but for the salt that has been added.

The *potato chip* and the *french fry* are perfect examples of the *double threat*. Take a bland basic potato, add the mouth-feel of fat crisping and you still have a bland taste; but add salt—liberally—and you have an addictive sensation coating a totally unsatisfactory product.

It has been computed that if we simply took the salt shaker off the table, we would reduce our salt intake by one-third.

Let's see if this is worth the try.

In northern Japan the people consume vast quantities of salt, about one ounce per person per day, which is about three times the U.S. average. They also suffer from high blood pressure; in fact 40 percent of the adult population are afflicted, and many die as a result of hypertension.

We know by this excess that salt can be a killer, so reversing the intake should lessen the problem, and it does! A very low sodium intake will reduce blood pressure, but it cannot reverse all the damage done. Research at the Longevity Center in Santa Barbara indicated that salt damage to the human system can be permanent.* They do not know the reason, but they sincerely state it to be the case. I believe we should carefully search our own hearts to see if the salt being consumed by our families is excessive and therefore doing permanent damage to their bodies!

Note that there are other causes of high blood pressure apart from salt—kidney diseases and atherosclerosis among others, but salt reduction is a step we can take for those who have it and also for those who shouldn't get it!

Let's look at some methods of taking out the excess:

Salted snack foods. Here we include potato chips, salted nuts,

* *Live Longer Now* (Today Press, 1972), page 70.

olives, pretzels, crackers and a wide variety of corn- or wheat-based party foods. They are all extremely addictive and all excessively salted. For good health, they should all go! In their place we can serve unsalted raw nuts and seeds that in their own right are delicious.

MSG. Monosodium glutamate is a thoroughly dangerous product. It is used to elevate taste sensation without being aggressively salty in its own right. MSG has been shown to produce possible brain damage in baby laboratory animals. Because of these findings, doctors recommend to their pregnant patients that they not take MSG until it can be proved to be safe. That comment is enough for me; there must be a better way to "lift" my food than to resort to an unproved substance. The use of MSG is approximately 40 million pounds per year in over 10,000 different commercially prepared foods. It's a neat reason to cut out four-fifths of our trips to the supermarket!

HYDROLIZED PROTEIN (HYDROLYSATE). Since MSG has been banned in all prepared baby foods, it is interesting to note that a new name has emerged as a substitute: hydrolized protein or hydrolysate. When protein is hydrolized (a chemical reaction in which a compound reacts with the ions of water to produce a weak acid, a weak base or both), the individual amino acids are released in free form—and one of these is MSG. So we now receive the same chemical through the back door!

SALTED MEATS. One immediate measure can beat two problems with one decision. If you ban everything that uses sodium nitrates or sodium nitrites, you safely edge out all bacon, ham, bologna, salami, pre-prepared luncheon meats, meat spreads, salted fish and frankfurters, and that's a hefty field. If you read chapter 4 on this important issue it may help you in your decision.

SOY SAUCE. I have had to look carefully at this one and must admit that my previous enthusiasm for the product* has been somewhat modified by my research. It can be used to fill in for severely reduced fat levels, but it's like robbing Peter to pay Paul. I recommend to you the 8 percent sodium soy sauce that needs refrigeration (you can buy it at stores that stock health foods), but otherwise I believe we should see it as a potentially dangerous source of salt addiction.

* *The New Seasoning* (New York: Simon and Schuster, 1976).

8

The Restructured-Food Decision

Let me first of all explain what I mean by "restructured" foods. These are foods subjected to chemical and mechanical engineering to make a new food substance. Let me give some illustrations.

COFFEE WHITENERS. The so-called nondairy creamers are derived from soybeans with additives.

MARGARINES. Oils made solid by hydrogenation, a technique that converts the naturally polyunsaturated oil into partially saturated fat. It was first used in 1920 to make soap!

MODIFIED STARCH. Many treatments are classified here, including blowing chlorine gas through flour to lower the gluten and to bleach and mature the particles.

POLYUNSATURATED DAIRY PRODUCTS. The University of California has found a technique by which, through feeding special grains to cows, they can bypass a digestive process and produce more than the usual 3 percent polyunsaturate level of regular milk. Students on a diet restricted to this "food" report an average 14 percent lower cholesterol level.

PASTEURIZED MILK. Much disease is eliminated by heating of milk to destroy bacteria, but we also lose some 90 percent of the enzymes, and *all* the proteins, fats, carbohydrates and minerals are altered. The vitamin content is lowered by 30–40 percent according to the temperature used by individual plants.

PROCESSED CHEESE. This is really nothing more than grinding up any quality of cheese, adding emulsifiers, chemicals, and color and forcing it into neat little plastic-coated blocks designed to fit the sandwich.

This list only skims the surface of what's going on, but it's sufficient to explain the breadth of the intrusion into our daily food. Let me now quote a paper published in the January 1976 issue of *Environment* (page 32):

> The FDA [Food and Drug Administration] now requires full disclosure of the "food value" of manufactured foods on the label, but methodology of food fabrication develops unimpeded either by scientific or public scrutiny.

Since you might feel this is just another jab by the environmentalists against the government, let me go on with the quotes, this time from *Bakery, Production and Marketing*, a trade magazine (vol. 7, no. 7 [1972], pp. 112–114):

> USDA [United States Department of Agriculture] confesses that it is useless to try to persuade the public to eat foods that are nutritionally good for them. Instead nutrition should be engineered into foods that the public likes. Frankfurters could be *beefed up* with protein and candy could be enriched with vitamins and minerals.

That was written in 1972; the action has already been taken, and many of us are apparently condemned to purchase these so-called enriched foods.

But what do the industry giants say in reply? Let's quote Arthur Odell of General Mills:

> You can't sell nutrition. . . . Hell, all people want is Coke and potato chips.

It is sad but true that the labels tell us only half the battle. You can add a chemical that has been classified as GRAS (Generally Regarded As Safe), but what about the method by which the food has been modified? The constant theme of food processors is to minimize the direct participation of nature at every stage. Our action as responsible "love-giving" home cooks is to *maximize* the direct participation of nature.

Therefore, we would do well to decide to sidestep the technology that tempts us with new taste treats, or new improved texture, or new superfast alternatives to cooking.

"Nature" may mean being "tradition bound" and "anti-progress," but we feel in our family that we should agree with the direction being taken by progressive technological steps before we participate.

Polyunsaturated milk, stiffened oil, gas-matured flour? No thanks, we'll take our food straight. (*Note*: see our approved food list on pages 75–81 for acceptable alternatives to these examples.)

9

The Artificial
Colors and Flavors Decision

Recently I caught a snatch of "filling in time" on a TV talk show—
one of those moments when the off-camera studio director mimes a
stretch by pulling some invisible elastic material out slowly with his
fingertips, the silent plea to extend the conversation.

Into this video void words were spoken, ridiculous empty words
about cooking. The hostess was saying that she had "no desire to
cook" and felt she was a "klutz" in the kitchen. In that moment I could
see why the processed-food industry got started and why it is increasing day by day in its manipulation of our simple daily foods.

We live in a ready-made alternative society, for whatever bothers
us about our own limitations, there is an alternative or *substitute* that
gets us off the immediate hook. Each of these *decisions* provides an
escape from the real world into a technological dependency where
science takes over from nature. Within this situation lies the seed of
the destruction of mankind as we know it today. (Real life is grass-
roots stuff!)

Color and flavor are given relatively little consideration, yet their
very existence as *artificial* additives does suggest that there exists an
unexpressed human need that is somehow not met in all known
manufacturing techniques.

The heat and moisture and friction employed by machinery
causes living food to die. When food dies it loses color and flavor. So,
like a skilled mortician, the food technologist comes along with
cosmetics and brings back the bloom of life, then adds a perfume that
suggests the living plant.

56

We, as consumers, have senses to warn us of dead food; a lifeless gray-green color and sour smell will warn us to stay clear. But when we see the corpse in its cardboard coffin we don't see or smell death; we see a surface appeal and we are tricked. This is why the words "artificial color" and "artificial flavor" are so dangerous—not just because of their toxic potential but because their use encourages us to eat dead food.

In the U.S. we spend over sixty billion dollars annually on prepared foods. In 1971 we crossed over into the era of buying more dead than live food—or, if you like, we accepted the fact that we preferred to have our food "touched" before we ate it.

In the "touching" process we have added over 3000 chemicals whose gross weight exceeds 800 million pounds. That means that you and I and our families could consume about 4½ pounds of mixed chemicals a year, and the mix is totally beyond our control, if we buy dead food!

Did you know that over 1000 of these chemicals have never been tested as possible causes of cancer, genetic damage or birth defects? Experts have decided that they may be accepted (without testing) as GRAS, a term meaning Generally Regarded As Safe!

Let's look at how this determination is reached.

Scientists used to believe that our bodies were able to detoxify poisonous substances absorbed through consumption and that toxic substances were broken down into less toxic elements in the digestive process. Now they aren't so sure, especially as our chemicals become more complex and the numbers so enormous. For example, there are two chemicals that are known to *increase* when "broken down" from one original cyclamate.

It is impossible—there are no known scientific methods available to us—to determine the synergistic effects (the effects of multiple chemicals upon each other at one meal) of our daily dose of chemicals (about five grams).

The tests applied to animals are not accurate enough for our protection. The Food and Agriculture Organization (FAO) and the World Health Organization (WHO) of the United Nations have warned against animal tests as total proof of nontoxicity.

In the case of Thalidomide, women turned out to be sixty times as sensitive as the test mice and seven hundred times as sensitive as hamsters. Beta-naphthylamine failed repeatedly to indicate cancer-inciting properties when applied to animals; yet we now know it to be one of the most active cancer-inciting chemicals.

Let's look specifically at color.

The artificial colors we use all come from coal-tar dyes. In 1900 there were eighty coal-tar dyes in use. In 1906, seventy-three were banned from food use, and of the seven left, a further four were believed dangerous.

In the ensuing years some were added. In 1950, a further eight were deleted because of new legislation introduced that placed the responsibility squarely upon the industry. The Certified Food Color Industry Committee, composed of manufacturers of 90 percent of the colors made in the U.S., then *modified* the regulations* with the FDA and established "safe" limits of certain colors.

I feel we need to know the manner in which these regulations are applied, so here is the story of "#2 Red (Azo) Amaranth."

"Big Red" is the Number One star of the food colors. He crops up in candy, pet food, dessert powders, baked goods, sausages, ice cream, sherbet, dairy products, cereals, maraschino cherries, snack foods.

He is hard to avoid!

In 1968, studies conducted in the Soviet Union indicated it was cancer producing, and in 1971 Soviet scientists further established that it caused birth defects. Also in 1971, the FDA ordered a reduction in its use and called for a report by October 31.

The FDA confirmed Soviet reports and added that the Big Red tests also indicated that *malformed fetuses* could be added to his credit. So did the FDA ban it? No they didn't! They requested the National Academy of Sciences–National Research Council to furnish a report. In the interim, Big Red continues to be a tool in the hands of our food morticians.

"A little rouge to the cheeks."

"A drop of #2 Red (Azo) Amaranth to the jam." It's really all the same!

Lest we dispose of artificial flavors without sufficient exposure, let's look at one aspect of the regulations that bring us into the scientific aroma zone. Prior to 1958, flavors could be accepted as being "safe" if they lived up to these criteria: (1) By experience based on common use in food. (2) By scientific procedure.

* Amendment 1960, Public Law 86-618.

The experience clause was a problem, because a well-known flavor called Coumarin was found to cause liver damage in rats and dogs and was banned after seventy-five years of use! Also, Safrole, used in root beer, was found to be a potent cause of cancer of the liver in rats and dogs; it also was banned.

FEMA (Food Extract Manufacturers Association) reviewed over 1300 substances. They admitted that some 100–200 may need to be dropped; 343 were granted time to be tested (while still being used in our food); 662 were "considered to be safe." And 191 were given an unconditional "white list" approval.

Look at the figures again:

191	White list approved
662	Generally regarded as safe
343	Innocent until proved guilty
100–200	To be banned at some future time

This is the overall picture you look at when you read on the food label, "artificial color" or "artificial flavor."

When you don't see those words, you avoid the potential problem and get yourself out of a full-scale controversy that even the scientists find themselves unable to resolve.

When in doubt,
Cut it out!
Learn to live on live food.
Let the dead bury their own.

10

The Chemical-Preservatives Decision

Our daily bread was once a "known" commodity, a staple, attractive, homely thing on which we could rely. We can now expect our daily bread to be treated to an incredible barrage of chemical manipulation.

We can assume that the following list has been applied:

Preservatives
Added nutrients
Antisprouting
Coloring
Flavoring
Bleaches
Texture enhancers
Emulsifiers
Softeners
Acidifiers
Sweeteners
Anti-foamers
Dough conditioners

The reason for their addition is logical enough: It reduces the effect of human error on the eventual product. Note please that it permits the error to continue, but it fixes up the mistake. We eat chemically remedied mistakes!

What man lacks in genuine honest skill he makes up for with chemical manipulation!

Let's look at a few well-known chemical preservatives so that we may better appreciate the problem.

BHA (butylated hydroxyamisole). The chief preservative used in our daily food. It causes contractions of the smooth muscle of the intestine in the ileum area (the bundle of intestine just under the duodenum that leads into the ascending colon).

BHT (butylated hydroxytoluene). This more toxic relative of BHA can cause metabolic stress, enlarged liver and weight loss with cholesterol and genetic problems. It is banned in Sweden and Austria. In Britain the Food Standard Committee took this action: (1958) Recommended an outright ban, but industry protested. (1963) Committee reviewed data and again recommended total ban. (1965) New evidence put to the test. BHT banned in all baby foods and quantity previously considered safe reduced by 50 percent. (1972) New evidence includes brain damage in mice fed large quantities of BHT. Humans thought to suffer chronic asthmatic attacks, extreme weakness, fatigue. Still in use!

NDGA (Nordihydroguaiarctic acid). An antioxidant. Banned in Canada, no longer GRAS in U.S. but still in use.

POLYOXYETHYLONE COMPOUNDS. The RDA banned their use but manufacturers went to the Supreme Court and obtained a postponement. Still in use in biscuits, cakes, cake mixes, ice cream, frozen desserts and pickles.

SODIUM CARBOXYMETHYLCELLULOSE. The U.S. Public Health Service warned, "If used in excess, such modification may have serious nutritional consequences for certain segments of the population." It is an indigestible material supplied as a substitute for normal food in an effort to improve texture and keeping quality or to lower calories. In other words, it's worth nothing, but it gives the mouth the *feel* of eating real food!

SODIUM NITRITE/NITRATE. Color fixatives used in almost all cold-preserved fish and meats. Nitrates and nitrites *may* react with secondary amines (an ammonia derivative in which hydrogen atoms have been replaced by a group of two atoms that act as a single atom containing hydrogen and carbon atoms) in the acid digestive tracts to form nitrosamines: one of the most potent cancer-causing agents known to science.

Once again you will note that there is a continual ebb and flow of opinion between industry and those who serve the common good of the consuming public. My reaction is one of understanding the problems that industry faces but still being realistic about where I am with my family. I simply do not want to accept anyone's word for it. *The least is the best, when it comes to chemical additives.*

If it means that the entire preserved-meats counter is suspect—then so be it! I am genuinely open to reason, but I will not sacrifice my body for the sake of my senses. I now look for the label that reads "no preservatives," and I consume the product quickly.

11

The Nutrification Decision

"The attitudes of the professional nutritionalists toward enrichment stem directly from their view of what constitutes nutrition."*

We first recognized vitamins when they were added to our flour during World War II. The simple assumption was then made that vitamins make the difference between good and bad nutrition, and this is still where we are today—but it just isn't true!

To explain this point, I'm going to take a very brief plunge back into history.

1530–1650: IATROCHEMICAL PERIOD†

A Swiss scientist named Paracelsus (1493–1541) stepped out of the alchemist's role (the effort to transmute base metals into gold) and began to formulate medicines and color dyes. Everyone started to look for the life process in chemical terms but completely ignored anatomy, pathology and physiology.

1690–1800: SCIENTIFIC PERIOD

This embodied all the previously ignored sciences.

1800: OXYGEN PERIOD

Together with new tools, chemical composition and weights measured.

* "Environment" Jan/Feb. issue 1976 page 29 by Ross Hume Hall.
† *Iatros* (Greek) = physician.

1828: Vitalism Ended

The "vital force in living process" theory was disproved when Friedrich Wohler chemically synthesized urea, a recognized product of the living process.

1834: Metabolic Period

Justus Liebig (1803–1873) discovered metabolism and was the first to clearly distinguish fat, carbohydrate and protein.

1890: Molecular-structure Period

The major molecular structures of carbohydrate, fat and protein were worked out.

1912: Disease by Deficiency Theory

Sir Fredrick Gowland Hopkins suggested that some diseases were caused by deficiencies in the diet. This was very hard to accept because Pasteur had caught everyone's attention by stating that "*some* diseases are caused by microbes." As is our human failing, we immediately translated this into "therefore, *all* are so caused." However, Hopkins' notion took root in some men's minds, and the business of classification began.

1900: Classification Period

To illustrate this, let's look at the discovery and classification of vitamin C. First a diet-deficiency disease—scurvy—was isolated and then a natural food that caused recovery—lime juice—was found. Then began the work of separating the chemical constituent that actually did the healing, in this case ascorbic acid. It was named vitamin C. Unless a system can be defined in which a single disease problem is identified with a single chemical, the nutritional scientist does not have a workable experimental system.

1900–1950: The Vitamin Research Period

Scientists were thrilled to see individual chemicals heal individual diseases, and much fame and fortune was waiting to be collected. The old alchemists returned to turn food into gold. The chemist began to look upon nutrition as vitamins and minerals and took no apparent interest in the fats and carbohydrates. By 1950 all the vitamins had been discovered and the gold rush was over. The chemists took one last look around, judged the nutritional sciences as having been conquered and moved on into the rich new fields of molecular biology and cancer research.

Since 1950, nutrition departments have declined in importance and have been left in a kind of backwater by the chemists. As far as most of us are concerned, we are left with an adequate measure of adequate nutrition, all neatly packaged under the Food and Drug Administration Recommended Daily Allowance.

But let's look at just one of their recommendations: vitamin C, 54 milligrams (mg.) per day.

If the individual to whom this is addressed smokes only two cigarettes a day, then all but 4 mg. has gone! If a nonsmoker, living in a high-pollution area like Los Angeles, simply breathes unfiltered air on a smoggy day, then he will be vitamin C deficient before lunch!

Nationwide we pump 200 million tons of carbon monoxide, sulfur oxides, nitrogen oxides, ozone, tar and particles of heavy metal into the air we breathe. Just for starters, we kill off vitamins A, E, and C. The dense smog screens out vitamin D and the chlorine in our tap water wages war on our vitamin E.

In our polluted society we have to deal with pesticides, optical brighteners, detergents, radioactive wastes, chemical salts, fertilizers, animal and human wastes and residues from toxic metals. On our "nonpolluted" farms we wage another kind of war against nature with over one thousand fungicides, pesticides and weed killers, not to mention the methyl gas and coloring sprayed onto our fresh, living foods.

Once upon a time it was scurvy, a simple disease healed by a simple chemical; but how do you fight the thousands of chemical insults forced one way or another into our bodies each day!?

Chemical nutrition has run aground; it has stopped its massive advance into the unknown. We have been given a scale, supposedly an adequate yardstick, but clearly it's inadequate; we are a nation sickening from the society in which we live.

In 1974, doctors wrote 22.5 million prescriptions for Valium, the wonder drug, a Band-Aid on our frantic situation. This chemical costs $50 per kilo in Switzerland; by the time it makes its way to you, the consumer, it costs $75,000 per kilo. Not a bad markup! Is it any wonder that the "brains" are racking themselves for new ways to soften the eventual blow?

We simply must not kid ourselves that the package that says "Enriched with 8 essential Vitamins and Minerals" is doing us a favor. It's a smoke screen for ignorance—the manufacturers themselves don't know for sure what they took out, so they are only guessing about what to put back.

Our family has had enough of things added. By the grace of God we trust we have made it through the Chemical Period into a new era in which, until there comes a genuine scientific breakthrough, we shall avoid the gray areas by heavily reducing our variety, regaining some old-fashioned skills and enjoying the simple things of life: the things God made, the way he made them.

12

What Is Good Nutrition?

It is perfectly reasonable to suppose that if one hundred well-adjusted, normal men and women were placed together in a room and told, "ten of you will definitely die within one year," not one person would feel that the statement applied to himself or herself.

Healthy-minded people feel invincible. Given an opportunity to guess at our potential old age, we clearly see past sixty, and most people expect to be active into their mid-eighties. According to the Census Bureau report on social indicators for 1976, published on December 27, 1977, we find that a woman born in 1974 can be expected to live to be seventy-six years old, and a male born in 1974 might expect to live until sixty-eight years of age.

But our life span is affected by the gradually increasing numbers of degenerative diseases—diseases that are not being matched by corresponding scientific skills in finding cures or ways of avoiding these diseases altogether. In other words, the way we are living is beating the medical profession to the finishing post.

Essentially, degeneration comes from what we consume, the amounts we consume, how we consume it, how we void what's left and how we move about in order to use up the energy we have received. Since we humans are vain, or made to be so by social pressures, we tend to look upon nutrition as a means by which we might have:

Slimmer bodies
Whiter teeth

Straighter bones
Better hair
Clearer skin

Item by item, this list can be correlated with certain mineral, vitamin, protein or calorie excess or deficiency, but none of these adjustments can be described as nutrition. Nutrition is the complete cycle. To discuss one without the other is literally to preach malnutrition, because the *whole issue* is not being presented.

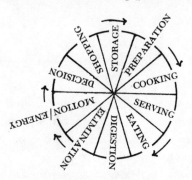

Let's begin with the cycle as a whole and take a quick look at the spokes that turn it into an effective wheel.

DECISION

Budget affects most families and often takes first place in *all* decisions related to what's actually eaten. The lower food budgets contain more potential for better food than those calling for more money spent without much control.

Vital good health for every member of the family should be the uppermost decision for the meal planner. Plan for fresh, whole foods with the accent upon vegetables, fruit, nuts, seeds, milk and cheese. Let meat settle into second place.

Plan to phase out all pre-prepared foods and beverages.

Decide to reduce the "dining out" experience, especially at fast-food-service and gourmet-styled establishments. Treat these opportunities as changes in routine rather than as an alternate food source.

Decide to eliminate all foods that cause you concern (subject to the emotional decisions that need family agreement) and don't buy *anything* that's supposed to be good for you until you *know* that it is.

Decide to give what you will save to a reputable world hunger-relief program.

Translate all these decisions into a shopping list and do not buy outside this list.

SHOPPING

Pay a special visit to your local supermarket for research only. Simply go, not to buy, but to read labels and absorb prices. Check *everything* that looks attractive to you. We have given you a list of chemicals that should wink at you like a Red Alert warning you not to buy. The government has insisted that you have the right to know what is in your food. By law it is now displayed, but if you don't understand what you are being told, it's all pretty useless isn't it? (See page 82 for "red alert list.")

Shop for the best fresh foods, and if possible, find an organic food source where they *guarantee* the food free of all chemical influence.

Shop within your consumption needs for perishables. It is better to buy perishable green vegetables at least twice a week. You might be able to crisp a wilted green vegetable in cold salty water, but you won't replace its nutrients!

Beware of the word "enriched." This word announces that chemicals have been added to make up for those removed by the manufacturing process. We suggest you buy the food *before* it's altered in the first place.

STORAGE

A rather simplistic message reads,

If mold won't grow on it,
Neither will you!

Hence your whole foods are going to be more easily spoiled than those you have hitherto purchased. Keep a waste list on your refrigerator. Actually admit to all that you have to throw out *before* it is cooked. In a study conducted in Arizona, it was conjectured that if the local figures were a reflection of the national scene, then each year we waste some eight billion dollars on foods that never get to the pan, let alone the plate!

What, we wonder, is this costing you?

Keep a list and you'll know!

PREPARATION

If you *must* peel vegetables, keep the peel and trim in plastic bags for each day and cook them quickly (five minutes at the fast simmer, not boil). Strain and use this vegetable broth for soups and gravies and for cooking other vegetables. After a short while you'll find you seldom go to the kitchen tap for straight water.

Wash all fruit and vegetables and cut or tear away all faded, wilted or bruised areas *before* you refrigerate. This helps to alert you to the immediate waste from certain vegetables, like leeks. You can also put bruised items into a priority-consumption bowl.

Don't let peeled, cut vegetables sit in cold water ready to be cooked. It is far preferable, if you are forced to prepare them some time ahead, to keep them in a plastic bag under refrigeration until they are ready to be cooked.

Red meats and eggs will cook better if brought to room temperature before cooking. The "younger" the meat, such as suckling pig, chicken, lamb, veal or rabbit, the more likely its spoilage in a warm kitchen.

Aim to have *everything* cut up and weighed or measured before you begin to cook. This simple technique sorts the Chef from the cooks. It's called *mis en place* (or put everything in its right place before you start). Any halfway decent TV cooking show will prove this point more than adequately—these performers don't have time to go looking for something or to peel a clove of garlic while the meat is already cooking!

COOKING

The more we grow to rely upon whole, fresh foods, the more concerned we need to be with retaining their fragile value. We make the decision to eat better in order to have vitality, but if we do all the right things and then dump it all into a pan and destroy all the advantages, we might be better off doing less work and go back to reading cooking directions on labels and popping vitamin pills.

I have provided a cooking technique chart in this book to help you with your fresh-vegetable conversion (pages 92–95).

We are trying to get adequate nutrition from the least destructive sources. We know that some forms of protein come complete with fat, which directly or indirectly means cholesterol, which directly or indirectly means some form of heart problem. Thus we reduce the protein from animal sources to a reasonable level: about 3½ to 4 ounces per day, total. We can look to vegetables, seeds, grains and some milk products to produce the major element that our bodies need.

Baking is virtually a thing of the past for our family. We bake bread (chapter 30), but that's just about where it ends. I haven't discovered an "adequate" cookie or cake, and the desserts seem to fade away when fresh fruit and cheese is served. A few exceptions are presented in the dessert section of this book (chapter 33).

SERVING

The least time-consuming and least costly element of a good meal is setting the table well. As a capital investment it may look like a problem, but think of the meals and the people you can say "I love you" to!

EATING

Our disposition at the time of eating is vital to both enjoyment and digestion. We simply cannot settle an agitated spirit with antacid tablets!

Eating on the run is an insult to our bodies. We need to settle down for at least ten minutes before eating and to remain seated for at least the same time after the end of the meal.

Chewing is essential, because the larger the piece of food, the more stomach acid will be required to dissolve it. All food should be thoroughly chewed. Compulsive eaters seek only mouth-feel rather than taste satisfaction; they can't gulp the sensations down fast enough, and to chew is frustrating for them. If you had to chew each mouthful twenty times before swallowing, would you find it hard? If you would, then you could be a compulsive eater, but rather than just read about it, why not chew on it and see?

DIGESTION

Digestion and elimination are the only parts of the cycle in which our bodies work independently of our efforts. Of course, we can make some additions when we have eaten or drunk too much, but the only truly effective *control* is to hunt down the transgressors one by one.

I do not doubt that my digestion is different from yours. I'm sensitive to different foods, and I *feel* my allergies. If I *feel* my new whole-grain cereal in the shape of heartburn, and take an antacid in order to cancel out the signal, then I'm likely to continue with the cereal *and* the antacid.

On the other hand, if I take nothing for my discomfort and suspect the cereal is the culprit, then I'll take action on the cereal. In this case I add milk to the grains a half hour before breakfast to soften the multiple (seven-grain) hard edges—result, no heartburn. I located the source, modified the use and avoided the condition.

We can all take this step, and frankly, we should, no matter how *addicted* we are to indigestion remedies. Indigestion is our body screaming for relief from abuse. We must listen!

ELIMINATION

When the beautifully prepared, balanced and well-chewed food has been swallowed and digested without the need of chemical aids, it still has to be eliminated.

Bowel movements are seldom if ever discussed in cookbooks, but we can't consider nutrition without completing the cycle. A clean, healthy, unaided evacuation of the bowel is essential if you are to experience vitality. Putrefied waste material in stale, toxic layers gets absorbed into the bloodstream and produces a full range of symptoms, all associated with exhaustion and causing us to reach for high-energy foods to keep the blood sugar going. Result: a fat human being with a poor bowel operation who is heading for chronic depression.

Bowels are aided by naturally fiber-filled or "sharp-edged" foods. The much-publicized *miller's bran flakes* and sharp-edged raw *sunflower seeds* are excellent promoters. They soften the waste matter and stimulate the digestive tract at the same time.

Keep a small bowl of raw, unsalted sunflower seeds mixed with seedless raisins in the kitchen to keep pace with your need to nibble. A few tablespoons of these fellows, well chewed, plus a tablespoon of bran flakes at breakfast mixed with other cereals, and fresh orange juice to drink should certainly get things under way, even in the most obstinate of cases. You'll need to drink more water than usual to get the best value from the change.

Of great importance to the proper cleansing of our systems is the fast. This simple means of deprivation has been muddled by many well-meaning folk. Certainly it is good to pray *and* fast, but the fast cannot take the place of a right attitude toward the subject of the prayer. What does happen, I believe, is that one ceases to be self-indulgent for a period. This freedom from self-serving combines with the surplus energy released by arresting the digestive process and produces concentration upon the objective, which is to petition God for a brother or sister in need. When a fast is conducted for cleansing purposes, self-interest is very much uppermost, and the three-to-seven- or even ten-day fasting period can be possible because we are convinced that the benefits to our bodies are real.

I do not believe that you can mix the two fasts. One is spiritual and cuts off our needs because we seek only that Father will help or heal our fellow man. The other is physical and is concerned with cleansing his temple (our body) so that we might be more effective witnesses for our Lord Jesus Christ.

I should make one observation here. The total exclusion of food for the purpose of losing weight is not and cannot be regarded as a fast. Weight loss can be achieved only by turning away from those foods that induced the fat in the first place. This represents a gradual healthy process rather than a swift, cruel pause in a continuing process of bad nutrition that is totally misrepresented as a fast!

MOVEMENT

The reason we need food is to fuel and repair our bodies as we daily move about our lives. The *way* we move determines *how much* we need to eat. Some people move quickly; they dart about. These people are usually thin. Other, taller, broader, heavier people move at a slower pace. Some people walk, others drive everywhere; some take exercise, others watch TV.

The fact is, we were designed to move on our own two feet, and while reclining chairs, TV sets, automobiles and jets are entertaining and convenient, their use has hastened our demise as a health-filled nation.

It is a *fact* that a person who takes exercise craves less sugar. It is a *fact* that exercise, properly conducted, can reduce a diabetic's need for insulin support. It is a *fact* that regular, meaningful exercise will reduce the pulse rate, increase the flexibility of the arteries and reduce hypertension. It's really up to you. Either you move your feet first or they'll move you feet first! (See our proposal in chapter 17.)

13

Highly Emotional Decisions

We have been through the lists of individual foods—the sugars, salts, fats and chemicals—and possibly made some "out-of-context" decisions. It's now time to plug these ingredients back into life and see clearly some of the complete dishes that become modified by your decisions.

I've listed those like a daily menu, because they are more familiar when couched in their normal interrelationships. Each has an A, B, C section that works quite simply.

    A. Factors contributing to bad nutrition
    B (i). Possible modification
    B (ii).
    C (i). An effective alternative
    C (ii).

You may find that my proposals under each B and C are unrelated to your experience or environment or personal taste. This is the reason the (ii) is left blank—for you to insert an idea of your own. You are, after all, the best judge of your family's taste.

BREAKFASTS

ARTIFICIAL ORANGE DRINK

    A. Sugar, artificial color and flavor, preservative chemicals, nutrification.

B (i). Fresh-squeezed citrus (orange or grapefruit). 4 oz. (½ cup) is enough.

B (ii).

C (i). There is no alternative to freshly squeezed fruit or vegetable juices. If some distress is felt with citrus, try vegetable juice, well chilled.

C (ii).

SUGAR-ADDED CEREALS (almost all commercial brands)

A. Sugar, restructured food, preservatives, nutrification (some), artificial color and flavor.

B (i). 1 tbsp miller's bran ⎫ Add to favorite
1 tsp. brewer's yeast ⎬ cereal as temporary
1 tsp. lecithin ⎭ "phase-out" technique.

B (ii).

C (i). Whole-grain cereal, including date "sugar," whole wheat, bran, sesame seeds, raisins, sliced almonds, wheat germ, lecithin, brewer's yeast, rolled oats. This can be purchased at a good whole-food store, or you can make it up to suit your family's taste. We find it easier to eat when it is soaked in milk in the refrigerator overnight. Add the B (i) "extras" to this cereal.

C (ii).

WHITE TOAST

A. Chemicals, fiber removal, natural vitamin loss, nutrification.

B (i). Change into "whole-wheat added" breads at your supermarket as a first step in breaking the tradition.

B (ii).

C (i). Convert to whole-grain breads that show the words "no preservatives or other additives" and "no sweetening."

C (ii).

DANISH OR SWEET ROLLS

A. Sugar, fat, some artificial flavor and colors, chemicals.

B. No halfway measure—simply replace immediately with the B (i) or C (i) recommendations for white toast.

EGGS

A. Fat, cholesterol.

B (i). The problem here is in quantity. We feel that an omelet is such a valuable part of the evening meal's variety that we prefer to receive eggs in main meals rather than at breakfast. We find that the proposals made for the grain breakfast are sufficient for anyone. Therefore we eat no breakfast eggs and have a limit of six eggs a week for *all* other purposes including one 2–3-egg omelet.

B (ii).

C (i). The egg substitutes made from grain products are un-natural, cosmetic foods, and we feel this makes them a figment of man's inventive genius, which means inedible!

BACON, HAM AND SAUSAGE

A. Fat, sodium nitrites, artificial flavors, salt.

B (i). Until such time as the industry discovers an alternative "cosmetic" chemical to replace the nitrites and nitrates, we have decided not to buy any of these products.

B (ii).

C (i). Once again, the grain breakfast with brewer's yeast, bran and lecithin added is really sufficient for our needs, so we haven't felt it necessary to look for any alternative.

C (ii).

SPECIAL NOTE FOR TRAVELERS

Before leaving on a trip, we combine sufficient cereal with the "extras" and keep it in a large plastic zip-lock bag. In this bag we carry a smaller zip-lock bag that holds enough for one breakfast. We then order empty bowls and milk or fruit juice and carry on as we normally do. There are no hotels, to our knowledge, that cater to eaters of healthy whole-grain breakfasts. The smaller pouch allows for discreet decanting in your room!

MIDMORNING SNACKS

CAKES, COOKIES

A. Sugar, artificial flavors and colors, chemicals, restructured foods.

B (i). Wayfarer Bread* or Lemon Yogurt Bread (page 202). We have not been able to find an acceptable alternative to cookies.

B (ii).

C (i). Please see our idea for the Biteables Box (pages 127–28).

C (ii).

LUNCHEONS

We have already discussed white bread, preserved meats with nitrates or nitrites added and artificially flavored and colored drinks no matter with what vitamins added!

Most people take lunch away from home—but need it be away from home influence? We have adopted whole-grain breads as our standard, onto which we pile lean, fresh-cooked cold meats, whole fresh cheese and lots of salads. We send cold fruit for dessert. The drink is now water supplemented by pure fruit juices.

On those occasions when we cannot influence the lunch, we order salads *only* and use either straight oil and vinegar or lemon juice as dressing. The only salad-suitable proteins we find acceptable when eating out are hard-boiled eggs, tuna, cold chicken and natural cheese. If the weather has "turned," we go for the *homemade* soup of the day, fruit and some cheese. If the restaurant has no freshly made soup . . . we leave!

---

* Sprouted wheat and raisin bread, the purest and simplest of all breads.

DINNERS

Our evening meals are now as early as possible. We eat at six o'clock, giving adequate vertical time for proper digestion.

To further aid digestion, we try to keep the evening meal light, especially for our nine-year-old, who goes to bed at eight o'clock. Lightness has meant reducing animal protein. Beef is out, except for our eighteen-year-old son, who is not yet fully convinced by our change of heart and diet. Andy's steaks are lean, very well seasoned (garlic, mustard, lemon juice; see page 134) and weigh only five or six ounces.*

Our meats range from lean New Zealand lamb to naturally fed chicken to fresh fish. We prefer to broil or steam our food and seldom shallow-fry anymore. We eat animal protein three times a week, an omelet on the fourth day and vegetables or soups on the remaining three days.

Our desserts are dramatically reduced to either frozen yogurt (without color or preservatives added) with fresh chopped fruit, a natural (homemade) ice cream or our No-Crust Apple Pie (page 233).

As you might imagine, all these changes have produced a series of interesting results.

Our food costs have tumbled by some 25 percent.
The kitchen time has been more than halved.
We no longer know the word "indigestion."
We have gradually reduced our weights to a normal level.
We feel a new sense of vitality and seldom experience exhaustion-induced irritability.

We know from experience that the change will not be an easy one, but we do encourage you to take a deep breath and start.

Be gradual, be gentle, love your family into better health. Swift action often results in misunderstandings and can be easily dismissed as a new fad, or a gimmick. *We are not involved in a gimmick.* This is a simple return to the days when the foods that God created were sufficient for man and there were no means by which our appetites could be stimulated by totally artificial means.

---

* Stop press: Thanks to the general cleanup in his food intake, Andy has found that beef has become isolated as the culprit causing stuffiness and nausea. He no longer orders beef.

The rewards are attractive: you can save money, share your blessing with others in need, spend less time in the kitchen, reduce your weight and increase your natural vitality.

But let's be honest—the temptations are also attractive. We can experience soft, luscious, sweet, delicious, crunchy, succulent and aromatic delicacies rich in color and flavor. We can be "sold" on our emotions—even in two dimensions we can be tempted.

If you own a television set, you will have seen commercials for *new* ice cream sundaes, for swigging down soft drinks with otherwise good foods, for the "fruit" drinks that are so good for us because vitamin C has been added to artificially flavored and colored water. You will see loving parents taking trusting children for a carton of french fries, fat-soaked and well salted. We see cakes that are so moist they must have been made from scratch!

Make no mistake, please: television is an extremely effective means of conditioning the human mind.

It is pointless to take a thirty-second slot for a carrot—we know what a carrot is—but sugared cereals need to be explained—not to Mother, you understand, but to the little ones. The smallest consumers cannot discern the difference between a cartoon character in a "play" and the same character in an ad endorsing a product!

> Consumer education exploits human feelings, drives and experiences, and seeks to direct these emotions to its own ends. . . . More important, however, it aims at incorporating the individual into the system emotionally so that he unconsciously styles his life according to the patterns of the system.*
>
> Small children are multisensorial; they do not think linearly or logically, and they jump instantly from one experience to another. Television stresses the audiotactile experience, an experience that harmonizes with the emotional make-up of small children.†
>
> The average child spends more time in front of the TV set than in front of his teacher and sees 25,000 commercials a year (220 minutes a week).‡

* *Environment*, March 1976, page 32.
† Marshall McLuhan, *Understanding Media: The Extension of Man* (New York: McGraw-Hill, 1972).
‡ "TV: Those Commercials," *New York Times*, April 26, 1973.

Five thousand of these commercials deal with food products—a total of 80,000 by the time a child reaches sixteen.*

We are now a nation growing up with our earliest instincts' being "adjusted" to a technological food manufacture—to respond to good-looking dead food is right, and to turn away from this supersold garbage is to encourage criticism.

In 1975 I was invited to produce a series of television capsules, sixty seconds long, in which I would talk about good nutrition to that huge, captive Saturday-morning audience in the "cartoon belt."

We prayed about it and felt that even though it was a transparent move to appease the consumer-rights-reactive parent, it might just help a few children to understand their food better. We proposed "messages" on good posture; on chewing food well; on seasonings; on receiving new food experiences (natural ones); on *not* having to clean one's plate; on candies' being a poor reward for good behavior; on unhurried breakfasts, better lunches at school and how to be a good shopping companion for Mother.

Then the Children's Programming people decided not to proceed with the idea. While I'm happy to concede that their decision might have been based upon my unsuitability, I'm also prepared to assert that the *content* in the messages might have been too rough on the junk-food manufacturers to whom they were enthusiastically selling time.

I must tell you that I'm pleased to be released by our Lord from TV. I know it can be used for good, but the avalanche of incredible sickness that spews from its silver screen makes it the single most dangerous mind-controlling menace in our home. You may well ask me why we still have it, and my answer is that I believe the Lord will give us the power to control it and to bless our whole family with the discernment to choose which programs will enrich our lives.

It's hard—but it's working.

* U.S. Senate Select Committee on Nutrition, Hearings, Part 3 (March 5, 1973).

14

Red Alert List

Make a copy of this list and affix it to a card or to your shopping-list book or folder.

It is designed to go with you, to help you to remember what to avoid if the Spirit of God has convinced you that while the scientists are in disagreement, you should avoid the controversial areas. In most cases the chemicals or restructured or refined foods listed have not been proved harmful to human beings, but enough evidence has been collected to suggest that there may be a problem—and *maybes*, to people who feel that they have life more abundantly because of Jesus, are not good enough.

Sugar (if listed in first 3 ingredients)
Artificial coloring
Artificial flavoring
Hydrogenated vegetable oils
Monosodium glutamate (MSG)
BHT
BHA
Nondairy cream
Nondairy creamers (coffee whiteners)
Processed cheese
NDGA
Polyoxyethylone compounds

Sodium carboxymethylcellulose
Sodium nitrates/nitrites

NOTE: Ice cream and other dairy products have been able to avoid FDA regulation for artificial colors and flavors. We strongly advise you to buy only those dairy foods which expressly state they are "pure—no preservatives."

This list is not exhaustive, but it's a beginning for you. Just add on each new chemical that develops its own question mark and avoid it too.

15

The God of Growth

I am convinced at this time that our fresh fruits and salads are as suspect as some of our chemically adjusted foods.

As I say this, I have a feeling of loss, of admitting that there is nowhere to hide in this miserable, chemically violated society. I want to have life more abundantly for my family. Jesus came so that I would really want this—it is a strong desire of my heart. I've taken steps to relieve my loved ones of the horrors of manipulated foods, and we have readily embraced the old-fashioned style of eating. But I cannot escape the polluted farm!

Chemists, employed in manufacturing, agriculture and medicine, seem determined to sidestep nature. Nature, it seems, is not to be trusted, so man uses chemistry to fill in for God. At each point in the natural cycle man has, with enormous ingenuity, come up against the natural "failures" of life. As we gain mastery over living matter, we are finding that each step forward means one step backward.

What we gain in the fields of the Imperial Valley we lose in the canneries of Santa Ana.

What we gain on the shelves of the supermarket we lose at the pharmacy.

What we gain at the medical center we lose at the mortuary.

Our nation is incredibly rich, tremendously creative, powerfully driven—but unbelievably sick! Cancer, heart disease, obesity abound; we are advertised into submission to perverted technocrats driven by the god of growth.

Personal income soon becomes a saturated goal in our society, being replaced by *corporate growth*—an ambition without end. Wall Street figures daily reflect the egos behind national growth. The stock market is the scoreboard for men too old to continue body-contact sports: they receive recognition by edging ahead of some old business-school buddy by a couple of points on the Big Board! Such alma mater rivalry would be amusing if it were not for the wreckage of our soil, our water resources, the air we breathe and the very cells of our own and our children's bodies.

Our nation screams its worship at the altars of stock and commodity-market boards, frenzied action by the priests of our culture, the middlemen with ticker tape on their hands while the high priests sit back in ulceritic splendor, nursing their hypertension and gout to the quiet hum of the electric golf cart as it carries them to a chemically "delayed?" death.

No, reader, that isn't prose—I really mean it! We must wake up to our real needs; we must stop the endless competitive drive that will finally defeat us all as we bow down to this god of growth.

I look up into the sky and thank God that he is there; I thank him that there is still time; and as I ponder on this truth I feel suddenly small and defenseless. I want to grow, but I want my growth to be toward God and not to be an end in itself.

I don't want to use my own will—my human chemical—to replace God's will in my life.

As I pray about these things, I feel God speaking to me:

Raise a garden, son. Plant some seeds and look after them. As they grow, some will fail; dig these back into the soil to encourage the others. When they are grown, harvest them; eat with gratitude, not to the chemist but to ME, their Creator. Share the excess without thought of return.

This, then, is the word about our families' daily food: A disengagement from the inventiveness of man as he seeks to force creation to meet fiscal standards. A simple garden, kept without chemicals to the Glory of God.

On these matters I hope to write in a future book, as God leads me to understand how this can be done.

16 _____

The Unexploded Bomb

Vegetables should be approached like an unexploded bomb, so fragile and so vitally important to our health is their locked-in goodness.

We have moved the star, animal protein, into the chorus and given the chorus of vegetables the starring role. To do this we now eat lamb, veal, chicken or fish on every other day (Monday, Wednesday, Friday) with an omelet on Sunday. This leaves Tuesday, Thursday and Saturday for the vegetable. Even on meat days we have small portions, about four ounces, and still rely upon vegetable-centered meals.

In order to plan for variety, which is *essential* to embracing of the concept, we need to divide vegetables into groups that will provide seven different types. One meal can then be made with one of each type, with a minimum of four. In this way we can get variety and adequate nutrition.

TYPES OF VEGETABLES

ROOTS: Beets, carrots, parsnips.
TUBERS: Potatoes, (Jerusalem) artichokes.
STEMS: Celery, asparagus.
LEAVES: Lettuce, spinach.
FLOWERS AND HEADS: (French) artichokes, broccoli, cauliflower.
FRUITS:* Tomatoes, watermelon, cucumber, squash.

* Many true fruits which are not sweet, such as tomatoes, beans and green peppers, are popularly called vegetables.

SEEDS: Peas, sweet corn, beans.

BUYING: If it is *impossible* to convert any part of your environment into a vegetable plot, then you will have to purchase your food some days after it has died. Here are some points to consider. Buy by type (the seven listed above). Your approximate needs for a family of four are:

Roots	8 oz. per person	=	2	lbs.
Tubers	8 oz. per person	=	2	lbs.
Stems	6 oz. per person	=	1½	lbs.
Leaves	10 oz. per person	=	2½	lbs.
Flowers	10 oz. per person	=	2½	lbs.
Fruits	6 oz. per person	=	1½	lbs.
Seeds	½ oz. per person	=	2	oz.

These are all raw, before-preparation weights and reduce by an average of 10 percent when ready for cooking and a further 10–15 percent in cooking.

Thus a meal consisting of

8 oz. carrots
6 oz. celery
10 oz. broccoli
6 oz. zucchini
_____

TOTAL 1 lb. 14 oz.

can be reduced to about 1½ lbs. on the plate.

Obviously, in our profit-conscious society, the farmer is interested in developing hybrids that can stand mechanized methods of distribution. The tomato is bred for a tough skin and plenty of flesh. It is picked green and ripens on the truck, or is sprayed with ethylene gas to hasten the process so that you and I might be pleased with its nice even color!

I need hardly add that all this is design for profit and not nutrition. We need to be alert to this problem. To exert the greatest pressure on the businessman we simply avoid *dull, lackluster foods, withered leaves or beans* and *unnaturally colored fruits and vegetables* and buy the best available by *type*. This means we stop buying celery because celery is on our list; we now write

2½ lbs. *stem*
2½ lbs. *flowers*
1½ lbs. *tuber*

and get the best!

The "best" has already been dead for several days, so it should be treated carefully.

PRE-PREPARATION

Since all store-purchased nonorganic fruits and vegetables are treated with some kind of chemical, we should get into the habit of washing our purchases before we store them.

The best method is to measure two tablespoons of hydrochloric acid to each gallon of cold water in your sink and thoroughly rinse *everything* you have purchased. Allow to drain and, in the case of leaves, dry them with a soft cloth or paper toweling.

Potatoes and hard squash can be kept without refrigeration, but all the rest are better held at 43°–45°F. in plastic bags or large glass jars.

PREPARATION

The moment we lay hands upon a vegetable with a knife or grater, we rupture cells and expose valuable vitamins to both light and oxygen. As we do this, the nutrients are destroyed. The longer we leave cut food exposed, the less of its nutrients we will receive.

It is true that some vitamins are not readily harmed by light and heat, but since they do not *gain* by different handling, I prefer to treat all vegetables the same when it comes to preparation before cooking.

There is a catering practice of soaking prepared and sliced vegetables in cold water before cooking. This stops ugly browning from taking place. It's a poor method and has no justification in the home, where it severely depletes water-soluble vitamins and gives free reign to enzyme action. If you must prepare ahead, then put the vegetables in plastic, exhaust as much air as possible from the bag and put it back into the refrigerator.

BAD COOKING

I shall begin by sharply reducing consumption of two well-known methods:

Shallow frying, as in the case of the Chinese wok or French *sauté*.

Boiling.

Shallow frying does two things. It exposes the cut surfaces to light, heat and air and adds unnecessary fat to a consumption rate already known to be excessive. For example, in the case of vitamin A it has been stated that "the combined effects of heat and the free access of air may completely destroy the vitamin A.*

Boiling—that is, covering food with water and raising the temperature to 212°F.—is a totally destructive method, especially when the food is raised to that temperature while sitting in the water.

Here I must tell you about vitamins and minerals. Vitamins are designed to control the body's utilization of minerals. They are the "highway police" in our system; but if we have less than our quota of minerals, the vitamins have nothing to do. Without highway police we can still use the roads and the body can still use minerals (though not too efficiently). But without us on the road, the police have nothing to do.

To this, then, I need to add the startling fact that the average mineral loss from vegetables through boiling is

Iron	48%
Phosphorus	. 46%
Calcium	32%
Magnesium	44%
Sodium	42%

These are hefty figures, a reminder that the foods we handle are fragile and need our care. There is no point in nourishing our drains!

---

* Stanley Davidson et al., *Human Nutrition and Dietetics* (6th rev. ed.; New York: Churchill, 1975), page 212.

GOOD COOKING

Stove top and oven can be used effectively: the oven for the tubers, some roots and squash (fruits) and for casseroled vegetables. All the rest can be treated to steam, low-moisture or pressure cooking.

OVEN BAKING. 300°F. temperature should be used and all foods cut down to the shape that cooks quickest—usually no more than 1½ inches thick.

ON-SHELF BAKING. This covers such foods as potatoes and hard squash. In all cases the root, tuber or squash should be cut evenly to present no more than 1½ inches of dense flesh. We brush a light coating of safflower oil on the cut surfaces. This helps to retain the natural juices and keeps the food moist.

CASSEROLE BAKING. This is defined as placing a mixture of vegetables in one container that has a *tightly* fitted lid and evenly distributes the heat. The *dofu* pan made of enameled cast iron does this handily. So do the clay pots we see in "earthy" stores, but you must check whether the lid fits.

Large lettuce leaves are put in first and can be used to separate the various vegetables added. Then the harder vegetables are grated and the softer textured are sliced, cubed or even left whole. The whole affair is then seasoned with herbs appropriate to each vegetable (see list below), covered and baked for 30 minutes. Tremendous stuff, especially without butter and salt!

STEAMING. The object is to cook swiftly without leaching out the nutrients. The food is cut into thin pieces and placed into perforated steamer baskets. Three different segment baskets to one large pot is a good idea, as each can be added according to the time necessary. Here is an example for parsnips, Swiss chard and fresh lima beans.

The water would be boiled and the lima beans added (they need 15 minutes). Follow this with the parsnips, which, when sliced, need 10 minutes. Then the Swiss chard, which takes only 8 minutes. After a total of 15 minutes' *watching and care* you have a marvelously cooked medley of fresh vegetables all in only one pot! Please be careful to cover tightly after each addition in order to exclude oxygen and retain the steam and heat.

PRESSURE COOKING. Vegetables can be cooked in one pressure cooker provided they have equal cooking times, since obviously you cannot keep on releasing pressure to add another batch. The pressure cooker is effective because even though the heat is greater, it cuts down the exposure time, and that is a decided advantage (see page 113 for further information on the pressure cooker).

Low MOISTURE. This technique is often called *waterless*, which is not strictly accurate. There is just enough water added to kick up some steam and stop the vegetables from scorching. Frankly, it doesn't make much sense when you compare the concept with steaming. Low moisture also means low heat, and low heat means longer exposure. Also, the direct contact between pan base and vegetable does cause uneven cooking. The argument is that the vegetable juices are totally saved, but I'm not impressed because the steaming juices are equally rich and valuable as vegetable drinks or future broths, stocks or soups.

At this time I must admit that it looks like a marketing method designed to justify the heavier, more expensive metal pans. In saying this I'm confessing a personal error, since I designed "low-moisture" selling pitches for my former manufacturing concern to justify the use of enameled cast aluminum, which was the easiest unit to produce at that time.

BAG BOIL. Thinly sliced vegetables seasoned with the right herb or spice *but no salt* are placed into heavy plastic boilproof bags. These can be added to boiling water by the bagful without any risk of losing anything. They can be added one at a time as with the steamer, and the exposure to oxygen is minimal. The bags can be rinsed and used again, so the idea is quite practical. It also reduces the washing up! Times are slightly longer than with steaming.

Now here are some methods for you. They are designed to *under*- rather than *over*-cook because heat is retained during service, and even on our plates this stored heat continues the cooking process.

In this next section you will find a table that you may wish to copy and to keep constantly displayed near your cooking top or range.

Let there be no substitute for real love!

COOKING METHODS FOR VEGETABLES

Calorie and protein count are for a portion of approximately 100 grams, or about 3½ ounces.

HEADS AND FLOWERS

	CALORIES	PROTEIN (GRAMS)	ACID— ALKALI	COOKING METHOD(S)
Artichokes, French	70	2.2	AL	Steam/Pressure
Broccoli	29	3.3	AL	Steam/Pressure
Brussels sprouts	47	4.4	AL	Bag boil/ Steam/Pressure
Cauliflower (*nutmeg*)	25	2.4	AL	Bag boil/ Steam/Pressure
Garlic	90	4.	AL	Seasoning
Mushroom (*chives, tarragon*)	16	2.4	AL	Raw in salads
Onion (*basil, thyme*)	45	1.4	AL	Pressure/Steam/ Bag boil/ Casserole

STEMS

Asparagus	21	2.2	AL	Steam/Pressure
Bean sprouts	35	3.8	AL	Bag boil/Steam/ Salads
Celeriac	38	1.7	AL	Steam/Pressure
Celery (*basil*)	18	1.3	AL	Steam/Pressure/ Casserole
Green onions	46	1.	AL	Steam/Salads
Leek	40	2.5	AL	Steam/Pressure/ Casserole

LEAVES

Beet greens	27	2.0	AL	Steam/Bag boil
Cabbage (*caraway seed, dill*)	24	1.4	AL	Pressure/Steam/ Salads
Cabbage, Chinese	9	1.5	AL	Pressure/Steam
Chard	21	1.4	AL	Steam/Bag boil
Collards	40	3.9	AL	Steam/Bag boil
Cress, garden	40	4.	AL	Salads

	CALORIES	PROTEIN (GRAMS)	ACID— ALKALI	COOKING METHOD(S)
Cress, water	20	2.	AL	Salads
Dandelion greens	44	2.7	AL	Steam
Endive	20	1.6	AL	Salads
Kale	40	3.9	AL	Steam/Pressure
Lettuce	15	2.9	AL	Salads
Mustard greens	22	2.3	AL	Steam
Spinach (*marjoram, nutmeg*)	20	2.3	AL	Steam/Bag boil/ Salads
Turnip greens	30	2.9	AL	Steam

SEEDS

	CALORIES	PROTEIN (GRAMS)	ACID— ALKALI	COOKING METHOD(S)
Corn (*paprika*)	92	3.7	AL	Steam/Pressure/ Bag boil Casserole
Lima beans (fresh)	128	7.5	AL	Pressure/Steam/ Bag boil
Pumpkin seeds	547	30.3		Added raw to dishes
Sunflower seeds	615	19.1		Added raw to dishes
Sesame seeds	584	17.6		Added raw to dishes

ROOTS

	CALORIES	PROTEIN (GRAMS)	ACID— ALKALI	COOKING METHOD(S)
Beets	42	1.6	AL	Bake/Pressure
Carrots (*thyme, nutmeg, mint*)	42	1.2	AL	Pressure/Steam
Parsnips	78	1.5	AL	Bag boil/ Casserole/Bake
Radishes	20	.10	AL	Salads
Rutabaga	38	1.1	AL	Bake/Pressure/ Steam/ Casserole
Kohlrabi	30	2.1	AL	Bake/Pressure/ Steam/ Casserole
Turnip	32	1.1	AL	Bake/Pressure/ Steam/ Casserole

	CALORIES	PROTEIN (GRAMS)	ACID— ALKALI	COOKING METHOD(S)
Salsify	89	1.4	AL	Bake/Pressure/ Steam/ Casserole
Water chestnuts	79	1.4	AL	Steam/Bag boil

FRUIT

	CALORIES	PROTEIN (GRAMS)	ACID— ALKALI	COOKING METHOD(S)
Avocados	185	2.	AL	Salads
Breadfruit	81	1.3	AL	Bake
Beans, green (*savory, sage*)	35	2.4	AL	Steam/Pressure/ Bag boil/ Casserole
Beans, (*yellow wax*)	35	2.4	AL	Steam/Pressure/ Bag boil/ Casserole
Peas (*fennel, mint*)	98	6.7	AL	Steam/Pressure/ Bag boil/ Casserole
Pea pods (*rosemary*)	27	2.4	AL	Steam/Pressure/ Bag boil/ Casserole
Cucumber (*dill*)	12	.7	AL	Steam/Bag boil/ Casserole/ Salads
Eggplant	24	1.1	AL	Steam/Bag boil/ Casserole/ Oven Bake
Okra	32	1.8	AL	Steam
Pepper, green	30	1.	AL	Bake/Casserole/ Salad
Pumpkin	30	.6	AL	Bake/Pressure/ Casserole
Tomato (*basil*)	20	1.	AL	Bake/Casserole
Squash, summer	16	.6	AL	Pressure/Steam/ Bag boil/ Casserole
Squash, winter	38	1.5	AL	Oven Bake/ Pressure
Watermelon	28	.5	AL	Raw

TUBERS

	CALORIES	PROTEIN (GRAMS)	ACID— ALKALI	COOKING METHOD(S)
Artichokes, Jerusalem	70	2.2	AL	Bag boil/Steam/ Casserole

	CALORIES	PROTEIN (GRAMS)	ACID—ALKALI	COOKING METHOD(S)
Potatoes (*basil, mint*)	83	2.	AL	Bake/Steam/ Pressure/ Casserole
Sweet Potato	123	1.8	AL	Bake/Pressure/ Casserole

Bayleaf in all casseroles
Filé in all casseroles

17

The Feet-First Proposal

If you don't move your feet first, someone will move *you* feet first!

There is absolutely no room for doubt in my or anyone else's mind that physical activity is a vital part of the nutrition cycle. We eat in order to produce fuel for movement, so therefore the way we eat dictates the way we move. The heavier the slower; the lighter the swifter (usually!).

Activity can be variously described, from breathing while asleep to vigorous athletics, but all forms use energy that we derive from food. Here are a few brief values per one hour of activity for me (185 pounds) and my wife, Treena (125 pounds).

ACTIVITY	CALORIES EXPENDED	
	Graham Kerr	*Treena Kerr*
Sleeping	87.55	57.71
Standing (light activity)	181.90	121.98
Housework	303.45	203.49
Eating	103.70	69.54
Conversing	136.85	91.77
Gardening (and weeding)	439.45	294.69
Watching TV	89.25	59.85
Writing	136.85	91.77

Edge the numbers higher and we get into another category of activity called by some folks exercise! Now, that word strikes terror into the average heart, and what a lie it is; what use our enemy makes of it. The truth is that the more energetically we move, the fitter we become. So let's stop looking at it as exercise and begin to view it as moving with vitality!

ACTIVITY	CALORIES EXPENDED	
	Graham Kerr	*Treena Kerr*
Dancing (moderate)	311.95	209.19
(square dancing)	510.00	342.00
Hill climbing	728.45	488.49
Mountain climbing	749.70	502.74
Walking (2 mph)	261.80	175.56
(110–20 paces per min.)	388.45	260.49
(4½ mph)	493.85	331.17
downstairs	497.25	333.45
upstairs	1295.40	868.68
Bicycling (5.5 mph)	374.00	250.80
Horseback riding (trot)	504.05	338.01
Running (5.5 mph level)	801.55	536.51
Swimming		
(breaststroke) 20 yds./min.	358.70	240.54
(crawl) 20 yds./min.	348.70	240.54

If we choose to sleep all day, we would get these figures:

Graham Kerr $87.55 \times 24 = 2101.20$
Treena Kerr $57.71 \times 24 = 1385.04$

Since one pound of fat equals approximately 3600 calories, I would need to spend a day and a half sleeping to shed a pound and Treena two and a half days. But since I don't sleep all day, it is more realistic to look at the facts.

7 hours' sleep	612.85
6 hours' writing	817.10
3 hours' conversing	410.55
1 hour TV	89.25
1 hour housework	303.45
1 hour gardening	439.45
1 hour walking	493.85
1 hour eating	103.70
3 hours' standing (light activity)	545.70
TOTAL	3815.90

I actually burn up some 3,815 calories in one day. When I take in less than 3,815 calories, I'm using up the fatty tissue that I've stored about my person.

We are directly related to what we eat and how we move when it comes to our physical dimensions, but what about our general health?

General health is determined by blood. Blood is the uniform substance that reaches throughout our bodies to carry nourishment. Any degeneration of the pump (heart) or narrowing of the pipes (veins and arteries) will result in the deterioration of the muscles and the skeleton they support and the brain that controls the whole.

The brain is vitally different in that it normally utilizes carbohydrates and not protein or fat. It does this in order to obtain its vital growth element, oxygen. Our brains use about 45 milliliters per minute, which requires the combustion of 80–90 grams of glucose per day. This glucose ordinarily comes from carbohydrate or from protein converted into carbohydrate during fasting or restrictive diets.

A great leap forward is taken when we exercise our heart, which expands and contracts our arteries, and may well slow down the process of heart and lung deterioration which is so common today.

Let me quote some worldly experts for you.

Young men on high fat intake did not increase cholesterol because they took hard and regular exercise. (Boston: Mann, G. V., et al., *New England Journal of Medicine*, 253, 349, 1955)

Unfit businessmen aged 30–49 years had 30–40% higher cholesterol than fit men of the same age. (Finland: Hernberg, S., *Lancet*, 2, 441, 1964)

Masai drink 10 pts. fatty milk per day, yet their cholesterol level is only 166 mg/100 ml. Considered due to their very high exercise level. (Africa: Sharper, A. G., et al., *Lancet*, 2, 1324, 1961)

London double-decker bus conductors had lower C.A.D. (see page 47) than the drivers of the same bus. (England: Morris, J. N., et al., *British Medical Journal*, 2, 1485, 1958)

Men in physically active jobs have less coronary heart disease during middle age. (England: Crawford, M. D., *Lancet*, 1, 827, 1968)

"Although it was once fashionable to decry exercise as a means of reducing weight, a combination of exercise and diet is to be strongly recommended." (Davidson et al., op. cit.)

Exercise may actually reduce appetite, *not* heighten it. (USA: Mayer, J., et al., *American Journal of Physiology*, 177, 544, 1954).

"45% of all adult Americans (49 million of 109 million total) do not engage in physical activity for the purpose of exercise. Only 55% of men and women do any exercise at all but 57% say they believe they get *enough*." (*President's Council on Physical Fitness*)

"For men 50–54 age group deaths per 100 were: No exercise = 2.08; Slight exercise = 0.80; Moderate exercise = 0.55; Strenuous exercise = 0.33. . . . Exercise helps to control blood glucose levels and this aids in preventing a hypoglycemic cycle." (E. Cheraskin, *Psychodietetics* [New York: Bantam, 1976], pp. 140, 141)

"Exercise should replace tranquilizers . . . patients who continued regular exercise on a long term basis demonstrated a 25% drop in nervous activity." (USA: Dr. Vries of USC, *ibid.*, p. 141)

I'll sum it all up for you.

Our physical efficiency can be measured by the body's ability to deliver oxygen to its tissues.

1. *Far-reaching*. Exercise develops *new* capillaries to feed the muscles, and therefore more blood reaches more tissue with more oxygen. This is called collateral circulation, and it's good news, because more blood is moved out per single heartbeat.

2. *Heart output*. Exercise drops the pulse rate from an average normal of 75 at rest to as low as 45 when long-term regular exercise is taken. This means a drop of some 15 million heart beats per year!

3. *Elastic arteries*. When a sudden call for blood is needed in a certain area, the arteries contract so that the essential supply reaches its destination immediately. The efficiency of this system depends upon the elastic nature of the arteries. If they are hard they don't contract and the blood meanders to its destination. Result? Debilitation, weakness and a feeble body. Exercise maintains elasticity.

4. *Brighter outlook*. Better circulation means more oxygen—a better-fed brain, brighter outlook!

5. *Heal quicker*. More oxygen in the blood does seem to enhance our immune system—the ability to ward off diseases, the ability to rebuild tissue and the ability to promote healing.

6. *Cuts fatigue*. Exercise reaches every sector of your body with fresh oxygen-loaded blood. Your fatigue level is reached after substantially more effort.

My view on all this is identical to the input factor of food. If I control carefully what I put *in*, then I must be equally concerned about what I put *out*.

I can (and I have done for years) spend most of my life breathing shallowly and sitting in a "light-load" state. I simply haven't been moving in a vital way, and I'm slow and feeble as a result. But I am God's servant, bought and paid for at a terrible price. I feel called to put things straight at both ends and not just regulate the input to match my inactive output.

One great problem I experience is the "calling" we have received at this date. Treena and I *minister* to people who have seriously maladjusted marriages. To this end we do tend to sit and converse or counsel for hours on end (calories used per hour = Graham 136.85; Treena 91.77) or we may write for hours at exactly the same rate.

We might feel that God must be served before our physical needs, but why not combine the two? Why not counsel as we walk? It doesn't have to be all the time, but it could be *some* of the time!

Then again, I'm concerned about my sleep, but look at it—I go to sleep tired and wake up tired. During my sleep my pulse rate is about 70 and my calorie consumption is 87.55 (Treena's is 57.71) and my breathing is shallow. No exercise, so therefore my body is tired! If I get up an hour earlier (six o'clock in the morning), meet some brothers and sisters in the Lord for a "walk 'n' run," then one shallow, almost comatose hour can be converted into one deep-breathing, oxygen-filled, blood-developing, fellowship experience!

As a sedentary type, I have learned one or two human wrinkles that I'd now like to pass on as *life* to you before you start.

1. *Get checked out first!* Years of ill use or misuse or disuse can't be reversed in a day and shouldn't be. Go see your doctor first and get him to give you his release. Doctors are so nervous nowadays about malpractice suits that you can be quite sure that they will be careful about such a release.

2. *Stretch first.* Any responsible athlete will spend time stretching out all his muscles before putting them to an ultimate test. "Now," you may say, "there's nothing ultimate about a walk." But there is, when most of your day is spent in a crumpled, bent-over shape. So S-T-R-E-T-C-H! I'm not going to give you instructions. Cats don't need a book to guide them, and neither do we.

3. *It's the time that counts.* We need at least 45 minutes a day

during which our hearts pound and we breathe deeply; the distance doesn't matter (other than the fact that it will get longer in the given 45 minutes each day). The secret is to get up to 140 pulse beats per minute and hold it there for the 45 minutes. That is a continuous load rather than the on-and-off loads of tennis or 20-minute physical "jerks."

4. *Watch your step!* Select a piece of ground that is flat and covered with grass. Pace out a track so that you know the distance you are traveling; but be careful not to run to distance, only to time! Don't run on concrete unless you have special roadwork shoes, and even then be especially careful.

5. *Stiffness is a sign.* I used to be an "evens" man in the 100 yards (that is, 10 seconds for the distance). Now, that was moving and I'm proud of it, but it was also 28 years ago! I suffer from "Walter Mittyism" about my exercise. I buy good track gear and sense that old "roar of the crowd." But let's face it, they roar for others—not me. I'm out there to get up to my mark as a middle-aged man, not as a competitor!

In my first attempts I really overdid it and limped back home with seriously stiff or sprained joints. *Please*, if anything hurts in your joints, then slow down—walk, don't run!

6. *Fellowship, not competition.* Allied with the preceding paragraph is the problem of beating a pal to the post. It's ingrained in us, to compete. But let me share with you; Jesus wants us humble, not puffed up; he wants us to share each other's burdens, not to add to them! All we need to do is get the pulse up to 140 and keep it there. So please don't run off and display your superiority. It isn't the Olympics, it's the Kingdom of God, and those who are first shall be last and those who are last shall be first!

7. *Buddies are essential.* The lonely athlete is out there because he is a competitor and must outdistance himself each day, but we unfit people are noncompetitors; we just want to have life more abundantly, especially as we grow older. Therefore it's good to take daily exercise with close friends and move at a pace suited to the group. The discipline of getting up early is severe, especially in poor weather, and we need a buddy system for it to work.

8. *Walk 'n' run.* I have found that the simple scouting technique is the answer. I begin by running 20 paces, then walk 100, then run 20. Gradually over several days it can come up to 100/100, then after some weeks to 100 running/20 walking; but remember—*don't compete even*

with yourself. Otherwise, your goal will be to do better and better and eventually you'll just run out of steam, or you'll find you aren't doing so well; and you will stop and that will be just too bad.

9. *Don't worry about early signs of fatigue*. At first you will be staggered by your exhaustion; you'll come home feeling terrible. Take heart: it won't last—the energy levels will gradually build up provided you are eating well, as outlined in the preceding chapters. Early general muscle stiffness will also leave you as you keep moving on. But once again I must caution you:

A. Stretch first.
B. Don't run on stiff or painful joints (just walk).
C. Don't compete.
D. Get your pulse up to 140 and keep it there for 45 minutes a day, 5 days a week.

We are being prepared, a Royal Priesthood for things to come within our life span, when some human beings' eternal life will depend upon our physical as well as our spiritual ability to challenge the devastating impact of God's growing distaste for a world in rebellion.

18

Love

Finally: What is love?

Love is found in our earthly life when we respond to other human beings' needs rather than considering our own position first.

Unfortunately, real love isn't a conditioned response that can be learned; either it's there or it isn't, and no human struggle will reproduce it.

Strangely, it is the absence of struggle that opens the door for the real thing. It is saying to oneself, "There is no genuine love in me. Everything I do is tainted with self-service: I do what I do so that others will love me!"

In this atmosphere we are literally confessing the truth, because the only goodness we can express comes from God; all else is our self.

Of course, this kind of response can be a terrible burden. When I first grasped the nettle, it stung!

Our family believed in reincarnation. My mother and father brought me up to consider it perfectly logical that any kind of loving Creator wouldn't force us to blow the whole deal on just one go-round. A Korean infant with gross birth defects just *wasn't* created equal to John D. Rockefeller! So obviously God would set it up somehow so that that child's soul would be rewarded in another life for its sufferings.

During the forty years in which I believed, there were many love opportunities that I somehow didn't pull off too well. I self-served my way, along with moments of guilt sandwiched thinly between thick slices of self-indulgence.

I am an only child, so I was indulged by my parents; yet I gave precious little back. I seldom wrote or considered them, and my belief didn't call for prayer in their behalf because I believed that their souls had agreed with the Celestial Administrator (The Keeper of their Lodge) on the location, type and style of their current life, in order to test their responses.

Briefly, the idea was that a number of serious obstacles would be neatly set up along our life's path, and the way we went about solving the problems determined our successful graduation to the next level of incarnation. The eventual "blessing" came when we had navigated each obstacle in a manner pleasing to God, called the Right-Hand Path. Any deviation onto the Left-Hand Path was bad news and meant a return engagement with the same kind of obstacle in either this or the next life.

The eventual right response neatly lifted us up out of the world schooling grounds and placed us with the various Keepers of the Lodges, where we began as junior administrators helping to program the other souls. The really bright boys who did superwell at this were destined for only a few earthbound visits. They had a special knack of doing the right thing.

Such "All-Stars" as Buddha, Krishna, Confucius, Jesus Christ, Mohammed, Gandhi—they were all quick reactors and during their last life were given teaching roles to help the slow learners like me. Their typical responses to difficult situations were set down carefully in sacred writings that would help me know how to respond. In short, the writings were a projection of God's intention.

I read the *Scales of Karma* and some of Confucius, and I heard some neat comments from the Koran and the Talmud. I grew up in England and attended a typical public school where we attended a typical chapel and heard typical sermons. I became typically "C. of E." (Church of England) and considered myself a Christian—yet I never read nor owned a Bible; neither were its contents ever discussed at home.

When my continuing self-love set me onto a Left-Hand Path, a state easily recognized because it felt so miserable, I would rake over what I had done, see it for the error that it was, own up to it (to myself) and resolve not to do it that way again.

Unfortunately, my responses to typical obstacles did not get better—I seemed fated to go the wrong way because it was easier and usually more pleasant. One day I knew I'd have to get it right, but in the meantime I was having too much fun, even if the predictable guilt would bring on some kind of regret after the error had been completed.

I was, in short, a failure in the moral field. But God was making up for it, I resolved, by giving me success with my chosen career.

At one time it was estimated that "The Galloping Gourmet" television show reached more people on one subject through the use of only one man than had been achieved at any other time, through any other medium, in the history of the world. The show was broadcast worldwide, and the rewards clearly made me the highest-paid cook in history!

It was hard to reconcile my private moral failure with my massive public success. I could only surmise that an unusual set of obstacles was being carefully arranged to provide me with an opportunity to take the Right-Hand Path!

Of course, "Right-Hand Path" was my personal definition of "doing good" or actually of "being good," for which, as a result, I would be personally rewarded.

There were no rules, only the sacred writings as loose guides to responses—but they were all so out of date. So I learned to respond to my conscience and adopted a simple credo: No act was a sin unless it went against my conscience. If I felt free to go ahead even though the society in which I lived disapproved, why, that wasn't a sin for me—only for them.

I had set up my own guidelines, my own means of communication with God, and those who shared my life suffered the consequences.

Our oldest daughter was using large quantities of cocaine, and we had asked her to leave our home because the pressure was too much for *our* happiness. Our son was learning the art of drinking straight hard stuff at fourteen in an exclusive private school. Our younger daughter showed strong signs of insecurity and unexpressed fears at five.

Treena, my wife, was hopelessly addicted to drugs prescribed to prevent her total collapse. She consumed vast quantities of Valium (in 1972 over 22 million prescriptions were written for this charming little tablet), Darvon (a pain killer), Efron (a super Valium) and Mogadon (sleeping pills). She obtained marijuana from our daughter and amphetamines from a relative, and Scotch from the more-than-adequate bar we maintained at our gracious country home. She took these "adjusters" in order to be able to accept the fact that I had been unfaithful to her: I was an adulterer: I had lied and cheated. I had stolen her dream from her—and she couldn't get it back.

Try as we did, we couldn't put our belief to work. Teachers of reincarnation explain this phenomenon by simply saying, "If we were to be given the understanding at the moment of our decisions, then we wouldn't *learn*. We would only be *responding* rather than learning, which would be too easy for us."

In December 1974 Treena was due to be admitted to a mental institution for a lengthy stay. She was showing every sign of a serious breakdown. On December 17 she went to a small church to "take the waters" and be baptized—"to see if it helps."

That night Jesus stepped gently into her life. He appeared to her as normally as you or I would stand, yet he was radiant and full of light. He reached out his hand toward her and touched her heart, and he actually smiled.

Treena returned from the church and took her plastic tubs of pills—all the Valium, Darvon, "speed," marijuana, and Mogadon— and tipped them one after the other down the drain.

That night she slept soundly and awoke to find herself changed.

Treena didn't go to church and she didn't tell me then what had happened, but she did pick up one of the sacred writings and begin to read. She started with the New Testament at the beginning and had gotten as far as chapter 15 in Matthew when God chose to speak to her in the words of Jesus: "Hear and understand: not what goes into the mouth defiles a man, but what comes out of the mouth, this defiles a man."

God said to Treena, "Watch how you speak to Graham—say nothing, do nothing, but trust me." She knew it was of God because she had peace. She was free of her three-year drug trip without a tremor; she was sleeping, she hadn't lost her temper once and she was no longer afraid.

So she remained silent and trusting, and read the sacred writings in order to know the God that had healed her and brought her peace.

I discovered what had happened quite by chance and was delighted to be in a peaceful place for a change. The children were fascinated and so was I. We watched her as she lit up our lives with her love. Three months later I was totally convinced that Jesus had stood before her, and I wanted him to stand before me and touch my heart. I wasn't hooked on chemicals. My situation was even worse; I was addicted to *me*!

I cried out to God to help me, but he didn't. In total frustration I yelled, "What do I have to say to you to know you as Treena does?"

The next words I spoke, it was as though he said them for me, in answer to my cry.

"Jesus, I love you."

Oh, yes, in the past I'd said "I love you" in the hope of getting something in return, and that was good old *me* at work. But this was different, because I wanted the old *me* to be changed completely and I knew no other way.

He loved me right back. I knew it as soon as I had said, "Jesus . . . I love you." From that moment I began to love others without the need to be loved back; but I admit to you that it wasn't like striking oil and suddenly up gushed love.

It's been a slow process and I've got a long way to go, but I know that my Right-Hand Path "goodness" has now been identified for what it really was—evil. For when I did something good, I gave myself the credit and felt one step closer to God. Now I find myself responding to obstacles as Jesus responded, and I'm grateful to see my selfish reactions gradually fade out.

So now the love I have isn't really mine. It's a result of wanting to have my old self-righteousness replaced by his righteousness. I want God's Spirit in me to respond, so I'm eager to give up as much space to his Spirit as I can.

In doing this I simply cannot take the credit, because all *I* have done is surrender. The good that I do depends upon the nature and truth and degree of my surrender.

Now, how does God want us to live? How does his Spirit want me to eat, and have I been able to pass this on without the old *me* trying to be right?

I know that if it's God, you'll get the message; and if it's *me*, you'll resent what I have said because I shall be saying, "I'm right." This will be me putting you in the wrong, and we won't get anywhere.

Through this book I just wanted to love you and to encourage you to enter into the Kingdom in which this family lives. I could do this only by sharing with you our real life. I could have preached Jesus at you all day and felt spiritually "right," but if you were not able to catch the drift of the Spirit, then that would have made you "wrong." That would have made it hard for us to be reconciled, and my objective to love you would have been defeated.

It is because of this that I chose to write about the happiness that my family is receiving because we came to live under God's Government.

Come through his gates and join us.

Graham + Treena X Kerr

JOHN 17:21.　　　GRAHAM AND TREENA KERR

Rejoice Fellowship, Inc.
P.O. Box 2727
Palm Springs, California 92262

PART TWO

THE RECIPES
AND
NUTRITION
CHARTS

SPECIAL NOTE

Recipes given include food items that this family has decided to exclude, such as beef. These are personal decisions and are considered too radical to propose at this time. We also want to experience this as "life" rather than lay it on you as "concept."

Author

19

Equipment

BLENDERS

Every year dozens of nifty new electric gadgets come onto the market. Most are used a few weeks as novelties and then gather dust waiting for the spring garage sale season. Some stay on and become part of the way we cook and affect the way our family eats. Of all the useful items, I believe that the blender is perhaps the most effective, if not essential piece of kitchen equipment that we can own. When purchasing one, look for these advantages:

1. The unit should be glass, *not* plastic. Plastic scratches and becomes insanitary, absorbs odors and retains them.

2. The bottom should unscrew for easy cleaning.

3. There should be a feeder cap on the top for additions during operation and it should be large enough to accept an onion.

4. The blades should almost touch the walls of the mixer.

5. The sides should slope down to the blades opening from the wide top.

6. The exterior control area should be easy to clean.

7. There must be an easy way to turn it off (*practice* this) in case of an emergency. Timers are a menace for this reason, and totally unnecessary.

WATCH THESE POINTS!

1. Keep your hands on the machine during operation.

2. Secure the top carefully each time. Top must be on when machine starts and stops.

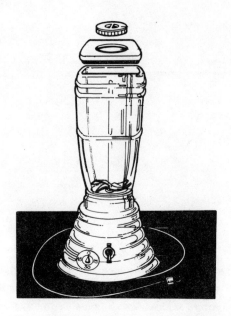

3. Learn how to turn it off quickly.

4. Don't operate over a damp surface. The motor sucks up water and may cause a shock.

5. If it overflows, turn off, mop up and carry on. With your blender, you can fix dozens of goodies in one-tenth the time you'd expect.

CLEANING ALUMINUM POTS WITH CREAM OF TARTAR

If you own a set of cast aluminum saucepans, you know they develop an unsightly tarnish, far removed from the buffed satin gleam they had in the store. You can remove the tarnish using cream of tartar —this can be found in the baking section in the supermarket. Do the whole set at once. It's easy and takes no muscle to speak of!

We mix cream of tartar and water together at the rate of 2 tsp. per 6 cups (48 fl. oz.). We make up enough to fill the largest pot in the set, then heat it to nearly boiling for 10 minutes. We then tip the liquid from one to the other reusing it for all the pans as they descend in size.

When the last pan is clean we throw the water away, thoroughly rinse the pans and wipe them hard with a salad-oil–impregnated burnishing cloth, leaving the oil to sit in the pan until the next use. The oil is never removed but simply dissipates when the pot is used; in this way the pan is "cured" with oil and heavy tarnish is defeated.

PRESSURE COOKERS

As you know by now, my changed attitude to cooking begins with the simple statement that cooking must never be a burden and that, if it is, then something's wrong!

One of the ways in which our daily food gets on top of us is in cooking of stocks, oxtongues, beans, etc., all needing at least 4 hours to prepare. One piece of equipment gets things moving fast: the pressure cooker, a device that simply *raises* the boiling point of water. At sea-level pressure (14.7 psi [pounds per square inch]), steam won't get any hotter than water's 212° F. (100° C.) boiling point, no matter how much heat is applied; the steam will simply dissipate. That's the situation when you are cooking with water in a pot without a lid or with a loose-fitting lid.

Put a tight lid on the pot, however, and the situation changes. Assuming that heat is continued, the pressure rises, and with it the water temperature. An increase of 5 psi raises the boiling point of water (and thus the temperature of the resulting steam) to 227° F. Add 5 more psi and the boiling point goes to 239° F. At 15 psi above normal atmospheric pressure (the maximum intended for our cookers) steam reaches 250° F, and food gets cooked a lot faster.

There are some old fears that the instruments may blow up. Let me explain that these were warranted at one time, but now the pressure cooker should be considered as safe as many other new appliances. However, be sure you follow directions for cooking time, clean out the release hole (*check it every time*), see that the plunger is loose on the blowout valve and listen to the "train" in motion. Also, cool first—open later (the Presto top indicates when it's safe to open). Check rubber gasket periodically.

Be very careful not to overfill! The makers recommend to only fill half with liquid and fill two-thirds with solids. This means purchasing a 4–6 quart size for even a small family.

One of the immediate ways in which this unit will bless your daily cooking is in the following recipe for stock.

PRESSURE BEEF STOCK

(30 minutes)

1½ lb. beef rib bones	*¼ tsp. thyme*
1 lb. hambone (shank end)	*2 bayleaves*
2 onions (6 oz.)	*9 black peppercorns*
celery (2 oz.)	*9 c. (4½ pints) water*
2 cloves garlic	

One of the longest, often most tedious and sometimes the smelliest job in the kitchen is making stock. All these minus points are instantly repealed by the pressure cooker. The 6–12 hour process is handily reduced to only 30 minutes.

Place the beef rib bones and the hambone in the bottom of a 4-qt. pressure cooker. To save as much space as possible, the bones should be quite flat. Add the onions, celery and spices and cover with the water. *Because of the pressure buildup, the pot should not be more than ⅔ full at most, and ½ full is preferred.* Close the cooker, build pressure to 15 lb. per square in. over moderate heat. Reduce heat and cook for 30 minutes. Turn off heat and let pressure subside gradually, at stoveside. Strain and bottle the stock and put it into the refrigerator to cool. When cool, skim fat and use as needed (for example, Onion Soup, page 153).

Yield: 2 qts. (extra ½ pt. water is absorbed and/or evaporated).

YOUR OWN SLOW COOKER

Slow cookers are all the rage but they do have two disconcerting problems. One is that you probably don't need another large pot, the other is that in some makes the center meat doesn't reach the needed 148° F. until *at least* 4 hours have passed. This means that some slow cookers are perfect incubators for bacteria. I'll try to take care of both problems by showing you how to use two pieces of equipment

for one job and provide you with a very inexpensive slow cooker that takes up very little space.

Just buy an aluminum, preferably Teflon coated bundt pan and slip it into your largest dutch oven. (Be certain to measure the opening before you make a guess purchase!) Pour about 1 c. water into the dutch oven and add 2 bayleaves, ½ t. thyme, 6 black peppercorns. Bring to the boil and reduce to a simmer (lowest heat). Add meat and vegetables to bundt pan according to the recipe (see below) and cook with lid on for up to 6 hours. The meat is cooked at 5 hours but will be in excellent condition at 6 or even 8 hours. Check the water level after 4 hours or place glass marbles in the bottom. They will rattle if the water level drops too far.

SLOW-COOKED BEEF CASSEROLE

2 lbs. beef chuck
6 oz. carrot in 1″ chunks
6 oz. onion cut in quarters
1 tbsp. naturally brewed soy
*   sauce (8% sodium)*
1 tbsp. tomato paste
1 tbsp. arrowroot

1 tbsp. parsley, freshly chopped
Freshly ground black pepper
1 c. water
2 bayleaves
½ tsp. thyme
6 black peppercorns

1. Cut off all fat from the meat and divide meat into 8 4-oz. pieces.
2. Put water in the bottom of the dutch oven. Add bayleaves,

thyme and peppercorns. Bring to a boil and reduce heat to the *lowest* setting on the stove; add bundt pan.

3. Place dry meat and vegetables with soy sauce in bundt pan. Season with pepper and cook for 4 to 6 hours. Be sure the dutch oven is covered during this time.

4. When meat is cooked, remove onion and place it in a small saucepan with the tomato paste over a medium heat. Stir and brown paste. Add the liquid from the meat, stir and thicken with arrowroot, which has been mixed with 2 tbsp. cold water.

5. Pour sauce back over the meat and serve in a casserole dusted with freshly chopped parsley. Serves 4.

WATER-BATH PROCESSING

One commonly used food preservation technique is the water bath. Jars of food are sealed with special lids and boiled for various lengths of time, then cooled and kept in a cellar ready for out-of-season use. In order to launch yourself into this rewarding skill you will need space and patience; you might do without the former but pray for the latter and it *will* be yours.

Equipment needed: a large deep boiler pan, a perforated disk to keep the jars from direct contact with the bottom, the jars themselves with lids and screw tops and a pair of jar tongs to lift the processed jars from the container.

If you have an electric stove or flat cooking top, you will have to buy a perfectly flat-based heavy utensil. If you want to process non-acid fruits and vegetables, then a large pressure canner is a wise dovetail investment at about $45 a 16-qt. unit.

The size depends upon the type of jar you want to use. We selected the 6 in. (1 pt.) size for our small family and need therefore 1 in. at the bottom, 6 in. for the jar, 1 in. for water coverage and 2 in. for the water to boil equals 10 in. total depth.

SOME TIPS ON WATER-BATH PROCESSING

1. Water-bath processing is used only for *acid* foods: fruits, juices, tomatoes, pickles, relishes, rhubarb, etc.

2. Nonacid foods (most meats and vegetables) *must* have pressure canning at temperatures of 240°–260° F. to kill any possible botulism spores. Boiling water is *not* hot enough. Remember that botulism is usually fatal!

3. Water-bath processing means heating the water to almost boiling. Prepare, fill and seal jars, place in the water and cover jars with 1–2 in. water over the top of the lids (fill with preheated water).

4. Bring water back to a boil and begin timing then.

5. When processing is completed, remove jars from rack and place in a draft-free area on a towel to cool 12–14 hours. Remove outer rims, wipe and store in a dry, dark place. Contents will remain good for several years.

Beverages

HOT SIPPIN' CIDER

As I write this recipe I'm looking out at Old Baldy, an 11,000-foot peak in Colorado. It's often at freezing or below outside in the winter, and a great comfort and pleasure is to put aside the usual tea and coffee or hot chocolate and brew up some spiced cider, equally good on a cool evening anywhere.

2 qts. fresh apple cider (unsweetened)	¼ tsp. whole cloves
1 tsp. allspice berries	3 in. stick cinnamon
	dash of nutmeg

PREPARATION

Tie spices in a small piece of cheesecloth. Measure cider and pour into a saucepan or heatproof tea or coffee pot (if using the latter, be sure pot has no coffee odor, and spices can be put in the percolator part where ground coffee ordinarily would be placed). Cover container and simmer for 15 minutes. Remove spices and serve with orange peel or plain in mugs. Makes 8 cups.

NUTRITION PROFILE

	CALORIES	CARBOHYDRATE	CALCIUM	IRON
1 c. apple cider	120	30 gm.	15 mg.	1.5 mg.

Contains small amount of B vitamins. Canned juice is poor source of vitamin C.

MAKING DECAFFEINATED COFFEE BY THE COLD-WATER METHOD

Coffee is now the six-letter dirty word and is likely to remain so. My family and I avoid any product that produces a craving when discontinued. If a withdrawal sensation is noticed, then we assume we are building a dependency, and our only dependency as Christians should be on our Lord Jesus. Here we have used decaffeinated coffee in a special way that eliminates the dependency but tastes good. It is also less expensive and quicker than perked coffee to make.

Select a good decaffeinated ground coffee and measure 1 lb. coffee to two 1-lb. cans of water (use coffee can to measure).

Take a bowl holding 6 pts., add 1 lb. decaffeinated coffee and cover with 2 lbs. *cold* water. *Don't stir.** Cover the bowl and allow to stand for at least 12 hours. Then strain through 8 thicknesses of cheesecloth. Use a colander at first, then gather the ends together and hang up over the bowl to drip. A good deal of the water will be absorbed by the coffee so that we should get approximately 5 cups (40 fl. oz.) coffee extract, sufficient for 53 6-oz. cups regular coffee.

Allow the coffee to drip through slowly. Place the extract in a bottle and cork or seal it tightly.

To make coffee for breakfast, boil milk and serve hot milk with the cold coffee extract on the side in a small jug. Each person adds coffee to suit personal taste. For a "black" cup, pour 3 tbsp. into a cup and add 6 fl. oz. (¾ cup) boiling water, stir and drink.

Keeps well for at least a week in the refrigerator.

---

* This is because decaffeinated coffee is super-fine and reassembled into ground bean form. When stirred, it breaks down into dust that clogs any filter.

ICED COFFEE FOR FOUR

2 c. 2% milk
1 tsp. vanilla extract
3 oz. (6 tbsp.) coffee extract
1 egg white

1 tbsp. confectioner's sugar
1 tbsp. nonfat dried milk powder
Fine-grated cinnamon

PREPARATION

Make a good coffee (see making Decaffeinated Coffee by the Cold-Water Method, page 119) double strength. Heat the milk with the vanilla extract and add the coffee essence. Place in the refrigerator to get very cold (always make up well ahead of time). Never add ice cubes; they dilute and ruin the drink.

For each pint of coffee/milk mixture, whip 1 egg white with 1 tbsp. confectioner's sugar and 1 tbsp. nonfat dried milk powder and place a blob atop the ice-cold coffee just before serving. This will look like a good "head" of whipped cream and it tastes good, too. Dust the top with a little fine-grated cinnamon for that extra touch.

OLD-FASHIONED LEMONADE

There is something elegant, Old World and loving about a large pitcher of ice-cold *homemade* lemonade surrounded by tall thin glasses. How this homely image has been ruined by foil envelopes of this and that slung together under a tap! The old ways are indeed loving ways and we want to encourage you to serve the real thing—for *their* sake!

4 lemons
⅔ c. sugar
5 c. water

5 leaves fresh mint
4 thin slices of fresh lemon

PREPARATION

Cut the lemons into small pieces, skin and all, reserving 4 thin slices. Mix the cut pieces with the sugar in a heatproof bowl. Boil water and pour it over the lemon/sugar mixture. Let stand for 10 minutes, no longer, or a bitter taste will develop. Stamp down the mix with a potato masher, strain and pour into a jug. Decorate with the mint leaves and the lemon slices. Makes 40 fl. oz.

COST PROFILE

If you buy lemonade mix making 64 fl. oz. (½ gal.) for 50¢, the cost will be the same—4¢ for a 5-oz. glass—but the flavor of the homemade is superior. Furthermore, the manufactured product is overly sweetened to compel overconsumption.

Replace the Package

GROWING GARLIC LEAVES

You can derive enormous satisfaction as a kitchen gardener by growing your own garlic tops. These tender green shoots will give you a mild, delicious seasoning quite unlike the robust bite of the bulb.

This is how we grew ours:

1. Clean small plastic or clay pots (be sure they have a drainage hole).

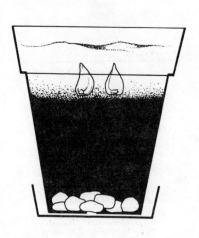

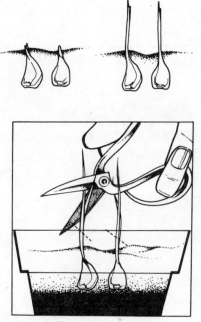

2. Cover the bottom with small stones.

3. Combine potting soil and enough water to make up a damp (not wet) mixture. Fill the pot ⅔ full with soil, then push 2 garlic bulbs into the soil round side down, pointed end up, and cover the bulbs with soil to within ½ in. of the top of the pot. Be sure to put something under the pot for proper drainage.

Progress should be seen after 3–4 days as a little green speck. After 6 more days the shoot will be about 2 in. high and showing the start of the second leaf. After another 2 days you can begin to trim off the outside leaf down to, but not below, the secondary leaves. We put the tops in our sesame/safflower oil and use it as a normal frying oil. It adds a unique and excellent taste.

CHEESE HANGUP

Making one's own cheese is a great hobby, and like all lasting hobbies, it starts out small and easy. In this case we made a cottage cheese with nonfat dried milk (NFDM) powder. All you need is the milk powder, a rennet tablet, some cheesecloth and a piece of string!

Prepare 1 qt. nonfat dried milk powder, using 5.4 oz. (1¾ c.) milk powder and 3¾ c. water. Allow it to come to room temperature or use lukewarm water to prepare it (at 70° F.).

To this milk add ⅛ crushed rennet tablet, and mix well. (The blender does a great job with no need to crush the tablet first.) Pour

into a glass, ceramic or stainless steel bowl (not aluminum). Cover and allow to sit for 12–18 hours. Next day cut up the curds into small squares, place in a large 4-thickness piece of cheesecloth laid in a colander, hang up for about 2 hours, then turn out into a bowl and mix different seasonings into it.

Yields 2 cups.

SEASONING 1. *¼ tsp. salt*
¼ tsp. chives
dash white pepper
¼ tsp. garlic oil
Good with meat and cheese dishes.

SEASONING 2. *dash allspice*
½ tsp. honey
Good with fresh fruits.

NUTRITION AND COST PROFILE

Whole-milk cottage cheese = 260 calories per c.
Dieter's cottage cheese = 128 calories per c.
Our uncreamed cottage cheese = 95.6 calories per c.
½ gal. skim milk = 73¢/yield 2 c. cottage cheese (4.56¢ per oz.).
½ gal. NFDM = 49¢ (3.06¢ per oz.).
2 c. bought cottage cheese = 59¢ (3.69¢ per oz.).

HOMEMADE MUSTARD SAUCE

This is a small sauce technique that can be made in an infinite number of ways, according to your taste. The saving over bought mustard is substantial, and it gives you your very own "house" mustard. This pungent sauce is highly acceptable to those who like to know they are eating mustard and who like horseradish, as it combines both.

2 oz. (⅓ c.) dry mustard
⅓ c. rice vinegar
⅓ c. horseradish sauce

1 tbsp. arrowroot
1 tsp. turmeric
1⅓ c. cold water

PREPARATION

Measure all ingredients. Boil the water and stir in the turmeric and arrowroot until thickened. Remove from the heat and add the vinegar, horseradish and dry mustard; stir until smooth. Place in small, sterilized bottles (baby food jars are great!) and keep refrigerated. Shake before serving.

COST PROFILE

Makes 2 c. for 75¢. Other mustards cost an average of 59¢ for 1 c., which means $1.18 for 2 c. = 43¢ savings.

HOMEMADE CHEESE SPREAD

Someone else has to do the work and they *have* to be paid. Should you pay them? Especially if it can reward your sense of creativity and remove your doubts about what they *may* have put into it to "keep it fresh"?

You might also like to sell them your idea! It's a shame that we have to consider "them" as a threat, but we feel that where we can avoid a package we are able to stand in freedom and to learn skills useful for a potentially troubled period that the book of Revelation promises.

1 c. milk
1 egg, beaten
¾ lb. grated cheddar cheese
½ tsp. dry mustard

½–1 tsp. optionals:
onion, garlic, chives, dill
weed, bacon bits, pimento,
olives, etc.

FIRST PREPARE

Grate cheese. Measure other ingredients. Beat egg. Plan and prepare optionals for special flavors.

NOW COOK

1. Heat milk in a double boiler over hot water. Combine egg,

grated cheese and seasonings and add slowly to the hot milk, stirring constantly.

2. Cook, stirring, for 15 minutes after the cheese has melted.

3. Cool completely, then store in a covered jar in the refrigerator.

4. Will keep for 2 weeks. Be sure to have at room temperature before serving, because it spreads better and has better flavor.

Yield: 2 cups.

NUTRITION AND COST

	WEIGHT	CALO-RIES	PROTEIN	FAT	CARBO-HYDRATE
1 cup milk	245 gm.	90	9 gm.	trace	12 gm.
1 egg	50 gm.	80	6 gm.	6 gm.	
¾ lb. cheddar cheese	336 gm.	1380	84 gm.	108 gm.	12 gm.
		1550			

1 lb. cheddar = $2.15.

1 cup spread = 775 calories.

1 tbsp. = 48 calories; 1 tsp. = 16 calories.

22

Diet Idea

BITEABLES BOX

Instantly available foods in the kitchen provide *nibble* temptation.

Usually they are empty foods: cookies, a slice of bread coated with peanut butter and a short glass of milk to stop it sticking! A potato chip—well, several because of the salt! A handful of peanuts or cashews. A "small" glass of a soft drink. It goes on and on—loads of calories with little else. Sweet, salt, sour, even bitter. The *tastes* are the driving force. Often we aren't even hungry; we simply crave a mouthful of flavor. Here, then, we present an idea called the Biteables Box. The box is plastic, has a snap top and fits into the refrigerator easily. It holds good snacking foods, foods with lots of natural flavor to help you over those moments when a cookie seems to be the *only* answer!

Paste the list on the lid of the box and seal it in with a clear wrap. This will help you to remember what to replace and remind you, "what's in it for you!" (item and calories content). When you feel tired, go for the protein foods and a cup of our "special" milk: nonfat skim milk with nutmeg—ice cold.

Replenish daily. Have whole fruit nearby and use one item a day.

	CALORIES	PROTEIN	SATURATED FAT	TOTAL FAT	CALCIUM	VITAMIN A	VITAMIN C
Apple, 3 per lb., one	70					50 i.u.	
Apricot, fresh, 12 per lb., one	18					900 i.u.	
Apricot, dried, one half	10				10 mg.	400 i.u.	
Carrot, 1 in. piece	2	trace				550 i.u.	
Celery, 1 in.	1	trace				10 i.u.	2 mg.
Cheddar cheese, 1 cubic in.	70	4 gm.	3 g.		129 mg.	230 i.u.	
Chicken, broiled with soy sauce, 1 oz.	38	7 gm.		0.3 g			
Crabmeat, 1 oz.	27	5 gm.		0.7 g			
Cucumber, 3 x 1 in. piece	15	trace					
Dill pickles 3½ x 1 in.	10				17 mg.	70 i.u.	4 mg.
Egg, half°	40	3 gm.	1 g.			295 i.u.	
Grape, one	3						
Green pepper, one quarter	4						23 mg.
Green snap beans, raw, ½ c.	17	trace				330 i.u.	
Mushroom, canned, 1 med.	4	0.5 gm.					
Orange, 2½ in. dia.	65					260 i.u.	66 mg.
Peach, 2 in. dia.	35					1320 i.u.	7 mg.
Pear, 3 in. x 2½ in.	100				13 mg.	30 i.u.	7 mg.
Prune, one	18					110 i.u.	
Radish, one	1						2 mg.
Raisins, 1½ oz.	40				9 mg.		
Shrimp, 1 oz.	33	7 gm.		0.3 g.			
Tomato, one quarter	10	0.5 gm.				410 i.u.	10 mg.

° Be careful not to overdo eggs; see page 77.

23

Seasonings and Oils

WHIPPED GARLIC BUTTER

Garlic butter is one of those highly appreciated extras that goes so well on crusty bread. It also has the distinct advantage of causing less butter than usual to be added to bread. In this idea we have managed to reduce the cost of ⅔ c. butter by 9.5¢, the number of calories by 410 and the saturated fats by 40.5 gm. And after all that, we've even improved the flavor!

2 oz. butter	*1 small clove garlic*
1 oz. (2 tbsp.) safflower oil	*1 egg white, whipped*

PREPARATION

Place butter with safflower oil and garlic in a blender and work on and off, pushing the mixture down the side of the blender with a spatula. Remove from blender and fold in the whipped egg white. This doubles the volume. Place in tubs and chill until ready for use. It is best used within the day, as the egg can gradually separate.

NUTRITION AND COST PROFILE

	CALO-RIES	SATU-RATED FAT	UNSATU-RATED FAT	CAL-CIUM	VITA-MIN A	COST
Butter, 2 oz. (½ stick)	405	25.5 gm.	16.5 gm.	11.5 mg.	1975 i.u.	
Oil, 1 oz. (2 tbsp.)	250	2 gm.	24 gm.			
1 egg white	15			3 mg.		
Total	670	27.5 gm.	40.5 gm.	14.5 mg.	1975 i.u.	22 ¢
⅔ cup regular butter*	1080	68 gm.	41 gm.			32.5¢
⅔ cup whipped butter (bought)	720	45 gm.	30 gm.			39.2¢

* Calorie savings = 410 calories total volume of our butter compared to regular butter.

SAUSAGE 'N' CARDAMOM

Cardamom is a spice native to India, but we get some quantity from Guatemala and Sri Lanka as well. We know that it grew in the garden of the king of Babylon in 721 B.C. It is used in some cosmetics today. The plant is a member of the ginger family, and the spice comes in the pod, or decorticated (pod off), or ground. It is good as a breath freshener. Used as a principal spice in Danish pastries, it is also good in pickles, grape jelly, fruit punch, fruit pies, and important in curry powder. We use it to bring sausage to life in this great breakfast recipe.

1 lb. link sausage　　　　　　*2 tomatoes*
in the casing, 16 per pound　　*ground cardamom*

PREPARATION

1. Fry sausages in a pan until lightly brown and cooked through.
2. Remove sausages and drain well. Make a lengthwise slit down each sausage. Sprinkle the tops gently with cardamom.
3. Skin and core 2 tomatoes, chop finely and spread over the top of the sausages, which have been placed in an ovenproof shallow dish.
4. Place the pan under the broiler for 5 minutes and serve immediately. Serves 4.

NUTRITION AND COST PROFILE

1 lb. sausage links (16/lb.) costs $1.66. From ½ lb., ¼ c. grease was drained off. This left 4⅛ oz. sausage meat. Therefore, 1 lb. will yield 8¼ oz. meat, and each person gets 2 1/16 oz. at the rate of 65 calories/link (4 links per serving is 260 calories per serving). One serving is 9.6 gm. protein and 22 gm. fat.

YOUR OWN LIGHT CURRY POWDER

Some folks like to be different. I suppose I'm one of them, because I just love the idea of making up my very own curry powder. Try the blend and add or subtract until you have it right for *you!*

1 tbsp. ground turmeric
1 tbsp. ground cumin
2 tbsp. coriander seed
1 tbsp. ground ginger
1 tbsp. ground white
  peppercorns
2 tsp. hot chili powder or
  hot dried chillies

2 tsp. ground cardamom
2 tsp. mace
1 tsp. mustard seed
½ tsp. ground cloves
1 tsp. poppy seeds
1 bayleaf
1 tsp. fenugreek

PREPARATION

1. Place all ingredients in a blender and whir on highest speed until finely ground (on and off repeatedly for a total time of 1½–2 minutes).

2. Store in small airtight jars in a dark place. This is very mild. For extra heat, add more chillies, cayenne pepper or ground mustard seed. Makes ½ c. dry powder.

THE GLAZED LOOK

Now that the "pump" has largely replaced the aerosol can, we can thoroughly clean the unit and use it for a wild idea—a low-calorie, highly flavored "mist" of seasoned oil that gives a surface sparkle to your food, bringing out the highlights without stirring in gobs of butter.

½ c. safflower oil
2 cloves garlic, crushed
½ tsp. thyme

4 bayleaves
peel of ¼ lemon, unblanched
2 tsp. grated fresh ginger
½ tsp. salt

PREPARATION

1. Measure or prepare all ingredients first.

2. Gently boil in a small saucepan all ingredients, except the salt, for 30 minutes, uncovered.

3. Strain through a cheesecloth, add salt and stir to dissolve.

4. Place in a spray atomizer and spray over a cooked, unseasoned steak, just before serving.

NUTRITION PROFILE

One squirt equals ¼ tsp. which equals 10.4 calories (1 tsp. butter equals 33.3 calories).

HOW TO COOK WITH GRAPE JUICE INSTEAD OF WINE

We would invite you to try the following classic recipe (adjusted to reduce fat) with grape juice instead of wine. Please keep an open mind. I'm delighted with the result, but perhaps I'm partial!

BOEUF BOURGUIGNON (SUPER CHUNK)

1½ lbs. center-cut beef chuck
8 small onions
16 fl. oz. beef stock
2 cloves garlic
1 large carrot
1 tbsp. sesame/safflower oil
2 oz. (¼ c.) tomato paste
2 tbsp. soy sauce (8% sodium)
4 fl oz. red grape juice

1 tsp. cold strong tea
bouquet garni
freshly ground salt
freshly ground pepper
16 small mushrooms
2 tsp. rice vinegar
arrowroot (optional)
chopped parsley

FIRST PREPARE

Cut beef into 4 6-oz. steaks (or 8 3-oz. chunks). Peel onions, make beef stock. Peel and mash garlic, peel and dice carrot in large pieces.

NOW COOK

1. Pour oil into a large dutch oven and heat. When hot add onions and carrot and brown. Remove vegetables and ham and reserve.

2. Add meat and brown well on all sides. Add tomato paste, brown. Add soy sauce and red grape juice and tea, stock, garlic, and *bouquet garni*. Season with salt and pepper (go lightly on the salt, since some is already in soy sauce). Cover and simmer for 1½ hours.

3. Add onions and carrot and simmer for ¾ hour longer.

4. Add mushrooms and cook for a further 15 minutes. Add rice vinegar and stir, removing from the heat. Thicken with arrowroot, if necessary. Serve dusted with chopped parsley. Serves 4.

NUTRITION PROFILE

	CALO-RIES	PRO-TEIN	FAT	CARBO-HYDRATE
1½ lbs. beef chuck	1344	211.2 gm.	48 gm.	
8 onions	80	2 gm.		20 gm.
16 mushrooms	40	5 gm.		6 gm.
16 oz. stock	16	2 gm.		
2 oz. tomato paste	60			16 gm.
4 oz. grape juice	83	0.5 gm.		21 gm.
1 carrot	20	1 gm.		5 gm.
1 tbsp. oil	125		14 gm.	
	1768			

Serves 4 at 442 calories per serving.

REFRESHING OIL WITH A POTATO

Cooking oil or fat can become clogged with flavors and discolored by burned bits of breadcrumb, etc. To "repair" the oil, clean it up and have it ready for further use, just add 2 oz. peeled sliced potato cut ¼ in. thick to each cup of oil. Add potato when oil is cold and gradually bring to the boil. Reduce to a simmer and let it stand until all the water has been driven out and the dark color taken up. When the water has left the potato, the surface of the oil becomes still. Remove the potato and strain the oil. It is then ready to use again.

STEAK WITH LEMON SEASONING IN LIEU OF SALT

For those on salt-free diets and those who are cutting down on salt, I offer a new seasoning idea for steaks and chops.

2 tbsp. French-style mustard
2 tbsp. lemon juice
½ tsp. powdered sage

½ tsp. ground pepper
1 tbsp. oil

PREPARATION

Combine all ingredients except oil on a plate and wipe the steaks in the mixture. Heat oil in a skillet until medium hot. Cook meat to desired doneness.

Yield: Seasoning for 4 steaks.

OLIVE OIL

We always looked upon olive oil as one of those saturated fats to be avoided at all costs. Yet it always held a fascination for its unique flavor.

In Europe they use freshly pressed crude oil, very pungent to the average American cook. By law, we insist that it be pasteurized when it reaches us. There are various grades:

Virgin. The first oil to be pressed from the crop.

Pure. Both blended and refined, which Italian experts claim destroys, removes or alters the vitamins, lecithin and unsaturated fatty acids.

Genuine Imported Virgin Olive Oil (how can you resist a title like that!). This product undergoes less modification than most domestic refined oils, it oxidizes less readily than most other oils, and has one great plus factor:

Olive oil is only 11% saturated fatty acids and 83% unsaturated fatty acids (oleic and linoleic). By comparison, safflower is 10%, sesame is 14%, coconut is 80%.

So Olive Oil Is In!

Sauces

HIGH-PROTEIN MEATLESS
SPAGHETTI SAUCE

One of the most popular sauces used from day to day is the Italian meat sauce served over spaghetti, meat loaves, etc. Can we make such a sauce attractive but *meatless*, yet retain the complete protein of meat and do it all at a reduced price and take less time? We achieved this by combining soy grits, sunflower seeds and peanuts. The result is both delicious and less expensive than meat. The fat is severely reduced, and for this alone it would be worth the effort for your family.

2 cloves garlic, mashed
1 large onion, chopped
¼ lb. mushrooms, chopped
⅔ c. ground sunflower seeds
½ c. ground peanuts
1 tbsp. oil
¼ c. soy grits (4 tbsp.)

1 tsp. oregano
1 tsp. basil
1 bayleaf
2 14-oz. cans Italian-style
  tomatoes
1 tbsp. Parmesan cheese

PREPARATION

1. Mash garlic, chop onion and mushrooms. Cover the latter with a little lemon juice to keep from going dark. Grind sunflower seeds and peanuts. Measure out the rest of the ingredients.

2. Sauté garlic and onions in a large skillet with the oil until slightly brown.

3. Add the grits, seeds, and nuts and stir over medium-low heat until thoroughly toasted (5 minutes). You may need to add a little more oil to keep the mixture from burning and to toast it well.

4. Add herbs, tomatoes and mushrooms and stir well to mix. Simmer with lid on for 10–15 minutes. Stir often. Serve over spaghetti or over zucchini for even fewer calories. Dust with the cheese. Makes 4½–5 cups sauce (4 servings).

NUTRITION AND COST PROFILE

	CALO-RIES	PRO-TEIN	FAT	CARBO-HYDRATE
1 tbsp. oil	125		12 gm.	
1 large onion	40	2 gm.		8.9 gm.
¼ lb. mushrooms	20	2.5 gm.		2.7 gm.
¼ c. soy grits	10	17 gm.		
⅔ c. sunflower seeds	374	18 gm.	31 gm.	13.2 gm.
½ c. peanuts	420	18 gm.	35 gm.	14.8 gm.
1 tbsp. Parmesan cheese	25	2 gm.	1 gm.	
2 14-oz. cans tomatoes	200	8 gm.	2 gm.	40.3 gm.
	1214	67.5 gm.		

Cost of our sauce is $1.80 or 45¢ per serving. Cost of one box spaghetti is 50¢ or 6.25¢ per serving. This serves 4 at a cost of 51¼¢ per serving, for 303.5 calories per serving (sauce) and 155 calories per cup of spaghetti. 16.9 gms. is protein per serving. Cost of protein sources is 10¢ per serving compared to 22 gms. of protein per serving with hamburger costing 19.7¢ per serving. (2 lbs. commercial meatless sauce costs $1.09. 1 lb. hamburger costs 79¢–99¢ per lb. Total meat sauce price is $1.88–$2.08.)

REFORMED SOUR CREAM

I'm ready to confess! The sour cream I've used in my old-style recipes would have been better measured by the bucket. Now I'm less free with your digestion (and mine), but I still like sour cream. So we set to work to take away some of its obvious problems—and we won. Please try it for yourself.

1 c. low-fat cottage cheese
½ c. buttermilk

2 tsp. lemon juice
¼ tsp. salt (optional)

PREPARATION

1. Measure all ingredients; set up blender; have a rubber spatula ready to use.

2. Place all ingredients in the blender and whiz on the highest speed for about 1 minute total, but turn off every 15–20 seconds and push it down with the spatula. It will firm up on sitting. Store in the refrigerator. Has the same consistency and appearance as sour cream. Yields 1¼ c. Takes 5 minutes to prepare.

NUTRITION AND COST PROFILE

	CALORIES	PROTEIN	FAT	CARBOHYDRATE
½ c. buttermilk	45	4.5 gm.		6 gm.
1 c. low-fat cottage cheese	170	34 gm.	1 gm.	5 gm.
2 tsp. lemon juice	7			2 gm.
	222			
1 c. bought sour cream	485	7 gm.	47 gm.	10 gm.
1 tbsp. bought sour cream	25–30		2 gm.	1 gm.
1 tbsp. our sour cream	11.1	2 gm.		0.6 gm.

Save 304.1 calories per cup; save 46 gm. fat and 26 gm. saturated fat.

Cost is 35¢ for 1¼ cups (30¢ for cottage cheese and 5¢ for buttermilk). One cup commercial sour cream costs 43¢ compared to 28¢ per cup of ours.

EASY BASIC BROWN SAUCE

One of the great classic sauces of all time is *sauce espagnole*; when reduced in volume it's called *demi-glace* or half-glaze. It's very rich, salty and delicious but it's also a killer in both time and nutrition.

Is there a replacement? I feel there isn't! But a good, tasty brown sauce can be made with little effort out of basic ingredients and be well received by everyone except perhaps a passing gourmet! Here it is.

1 lb. fresh, *ripe tomatoes*
1 oz. (2 tbsp.) safflower oil
2 tbsp. plus 2 tsp. arrowroot

24 oz. dark beef stock
   (see page 114)
freshly ground salt
freshly ground pepper

FIRST PREPARE

Chop tomatoes. Measure oil, arrowroot and beef stock. Mix arrowroot with 3 tbsp. of the measured beek stock.

NOW COOK

1. Heat oil in saucepan and add tomatoes, including as little juice as possible.

2. Sauté over medium-high heat for 5 to 8 minutes, until thickened and tomatoes are fairly dark brown, but not scorched.

3. Stir in beef stock and bring to a boil. Simmer 5 minutes gently with or without a lid.

4. Remove pan from heat. Stir arrowroot and stock to mix in suspension, then stir constantly and add arrowroot mixture to the hot liquid.

5. Return pan to the burner, and stirring constantly bring just to a boil.

6. Remove from heat and strain through a sieve, using a spoon to press all the juices through, but retain the pulp and seeds in the strainer.

7. Season to taste with salt and pepper. Refrigerate until needed, and then just reheat amount needed. Will keep about a week. Do not retain any longer, because after a week, beef broth is a good breeding ground for bacterial growth.

Yield: 3 cups.

NUTRITION PROFILE

	WEIGHT	CALO-RIES	PRO-TEIN	FAT	CARBO-HYDRATE
1 lb. tomatoes	454 gm.	100	5 gm.		22.5 gm.
1 oz. oil (2 tbsp.)	28 gm.	250		28 gm.	
24 oz. beef stock	720 gm.	90	15 gm.		9 gm.
8 tsp. arrowroot	29 gm.	85			22 gm.
		525			

1 c. white sauce has 405 calories. 1 cup of our sauce has 175 calories = 230 calories saved! 1 tbsp. has 11 calories.

Note: The classic *espagnole* has never been put through the caloric machine, but we feel it would be close to the white sauce and certainly must be double the calories of the sauce given above.

25 ——————————

Salads

CUCUMBER SALAD

A light salad before dinner at any time of the year is no surprise. It was popularized by restaurants eager to gain time to fix your order; but this one is unique. A salad that weighs in at 30 calories with dressing is in order for anyone—but making it taste as good as this does is something else!

2 cucumbers, sliced
juice of 1 lemon
½ tsp. freshly ground salt

1 egg white, beaten
1 tbsp. sour cream
dill weed

PREPARATION

1. Skin the cucumbers, if not freshly picked (commercial ones are waxed) and squeeze the lemon.

2. Combine the first 3 ingredients and allow to sit several hours or overnight. Drain off the juice.

3. Allow egg to come to room temperature. Beat egg white until stiff but not dry.

4. Stir sour cream into the cucumbers and at the last minute gently fold in the egg white. Sprinkle dill weed over the top and serve. Serves 4–6.

NUTRITION PROFILE

	CALO-RIES	PRO-TEIN	FAT	CARBO-HYDRATE
2 cucumbers	60	2 gm.		14 gm.
1 lemon	20	1 gm.		6 gm.
1 tbsp. sour cream	25		2 gm.	1 gm.
1 egg white	15	4 gm.		

Serves 4 at 30 calories/serving. Serves 6 at 20 calories/serving.

REFORMED BLUE CHEESE DRESSING

This fabulous cheese salad dressing is unknown in Europe. We have been working to create a new American blue cheese dressing so that we may move it into the realm of cost and nutritional reality.

We note that imported Roquefort is $5.00 per lb. compared with our local cheese at 55¢ for a 4-oz. package ($2.20 per lb.). Ounce for ounce, imported = 31¢, local = 14¢. When used in this dressing there is not enough difference in quality to justify the imported-cheese purchase.

3 tbsp. local blue cheese,
   crumbled
6 tbsp. plain yogurt
3 tbsp. cottage cheese

2 tbsp. mayonnaise
¼ tsp. dill weed
¼ tsp. chopped garlic clove
2 tbsp. celery, chopped fine

Combine all ingredients in a blender, except the celery, which is neatly chopped by hand into very small dice and stirred in.

Refrigerate and serve cold over salad greens.

NUTRITION AND COST PROFILE

The U.S. Department of Agriculture quotes blue cheese dressing at about 525 calories for 100 gm. (about 3½ oz.). Our value per 100 gm. = 145 calories.

Above recipe if made with imported blue cheese = 88¢ per cup (11¢ per oz.); if made with local blue cheese = 54¢ per cup

(6.8¢ per oz.). The cost of bought, prepared blue cheese dressing is 71¢ per cup (8.9¢ per oz.).

CRESS SALAD

As a child I was given special, very small, very thin brown-bread sandwiches filled with a wonderful spicy crisp green salad. We called it "Mustard and Cress," but more correctly it is harvest or garden cress. Mustard is a different seed which takes a little longer to grow, and therefore I am doubtful that they would be combined.

We purchased garden cress seeds from a wholesale seed house at $2.75 per ¼ lb. (4 oz.) package. This is much less expensive than the regular mini-pack at some health food stores at 1/16 oz. for 35¢.

We lay out 4 thicknesses of cheesecloth in a glass dish and cover it with cold water; pour the water off and scatter on the seeds. Scatter them thickly, touching each other.

Water with a household mist sprayer several times a day. At night cover with a large plastic bag and seal to keep the moisture in. When the green tops break out, give the dish plenty of sunshine in a protected place or put under fluorescent grow-lights. Keep watering until the seedlings reach just over 2 in. high. Then harvest with scissors and build wonderful *ultrathin* cress sandwiches.

NUTRITION PROFILE

WEIGHT	CALO-RIES	PROTEIN	FAT	CARBO-HYDRATE	POTAS-SIUM	VITA-MIN A	VITA-MIN C
Cress 3½ oz.	32	2.6 gm.	0.7 gm.	5.5 gm.	606 mg.	9300 i.u.	69 mg.

BLENDER MAYONNAISE

One of the greatest pieces of social status nonsense I know is beating mayonnaise by hand when a blender is available (see page 111). This simple device now sells for between $20 and $40 and can take the often difficult-to-make, time-consuming mayonnaise and make it in less than 1 minute. This is how it's done.

1 c. polyunsaturated vegetable
   oil
1 whole medium egg
½ tsp. salt
2 tbsp. rice vinegar
½ tsp. dry mustard
1 tsp. sugar

ADD JUST BEFORE SERVING:
1 beaten egg white per c.
   mayonnaise
¼ tsp. dill weed
pinch cayenne pepper

PREPARATION

Place egg, salt, rice vinegar, dry mustard and sugar in blender with ¼ c. of the oil. Blend at lowest speed and add a slow, steady stream of the remaining ¾ c. oil through the feeder cap, the slower the stiffer. Just before serving, add the beaten egg white, dill weed and cayenne pepper. This increases the volume by 3 oz./c. but must be added only just before the mayonnaise is used; otherwise it will fall.

COST PROFILE

Expressed as saving per quart, we get:
32 x 6¢ = \$1.92 = safflower (homemade)
32 x 3.5¢ = \$1.12 = vegetable oil (homemade)
32 x 3.5¢ = \$1.12 = safflower + egg white
32 x 2.1¢ = \$0.67 = vegetable oil + egg white
32 x 6.6¢ = \$2.11 = commercially prepared

RAFT SALAD

Western iceberg lettuce, the large-hard-crisp one, is so tightly designed that it can be cut into a "raft" between ½ and 1 in. thick and usually halved once again for a moderate portion.

The "raft" can be used to hold all kinds of decorative saladry. We use avocado, shrimp, grapefruit, olives and our light Blender Mayonnaise (page 143). The result looks impressive and tastes delicious.

8 oz. cooked, cleaned shrimp
1 8 oz. can pink grapefruit
1 head iceberg lettuce
1 avocado
salt and pepper to taste

Blender Mayonnaise
   (or ½ c. mayonnaise and 1
   beaten egg white)
⅛ tsp. dry dill weed
⅛ tsp. cayenne pepper
4 green Spanish olives
   (with pimento)

FIRST PREPARE

1. Steam shrimp in water and cider vinegar (¼ c. each) for 6 to 8 minutes or until a deep pink. Drain, cool and clean, removing the shell and vein down the back.

2. Open and drain grapefruit, wash and drain lettuce, peel and slice avocado.

3. Measure out mayonnaise and seasonings. Separate egg white and allow to come to room temperature.

4. Slice 1 (½–1 in. thick) layer of lettuce per serving and place on a salad plate.

NOW ASSEMBLE

5. Alternate avocado slices with shrimp and grapefruit. Continue until you reach the edge of the "raft."

6. In a small mixing bowl, fold together Blender Mayonnaise and beaten egg white, dill weed, cayenne pepper, salt and pepper.

7. Slice up 4 olives; reserve for garnish. Spread 2 tbsp. of Blender Mayonnaise over the salad in a line and garnish with one whole sliced olive, laid in a row down the line. Serves 4.

NUTRITIONAL PROFILE

	WEIGHT	CALO-RIES	PRO-TEIN	FAT	CARBO-HYDRATE
1 avocado	284 gm.	370	5 gm.	37 gm.	13 gm.
8 oz. shrimp	227 gm.	267	56 gm.	3 gm.	3 gm.
1 head lettuce	227 gm.	30	2 gm.		6.5 gm.
8 oz. grapefruit	227 gm.	100	1 gm.		24 gm.
4 olives	16 gm.	15		2 gm.	
½ c. mayonnaise	112 gm.	800		88 gm.	
1 egg white	33 gm.	15	4 gm.		

Salad contains 767 calories (192 calories per serving). Light, Blender Mayonnaise has 815 calories (58 cal./tbsp.)

Depending on the size of the shrimp, the cost of the dish is—large: 73¢/serving; medium: 50¢/serving; small: 38¢/serving.

SPLIT SALAD

The Split-Salad technique involves dividing those salads that can absorb without wilting a powerfully astringent dressing in which they sit for several hours (24 hours doesn't hurt, but 4 is enough to do the job). You then serve perfectly dried, chilled leaves with the marinated mixture on the side.

VEGETABLES

We find that these hard salad ingredients should be handled as follows:

Carrot, cut in very fine sticks.

Radish, cut in thin "penny" rounds.

Tomato, skin and slice thinly; select firm tomatoes for preference.

Onion, peel, slice in thick ½-inch rings, put in cold water and bring slowly to the boil. Throw out water and allow rings to cool slowly.

Green pepper, slice in very thin strips like carrots.

Cucumber, peel and slice fine.

Zucchini, slice fine, skin on, and drop into boiling water for just 30 seconds. Remove and put into the bowl with other ingredients.

DRESSING

2 parts white wine vinegar	*½ tsp. dry mustard*
(½ cup) (4 oz.)	*½ tsp. salt*
1 part sesame/safflower oil	*½ tsp. black ground pepper*
(¼ cup) (2 oz.)	*¼ tsp. cayenne pepper*
1 tsp. sugar	

Shake dressing well and pour over the prepared firm salads. Marinate in a cool place or refrigerate. Serve with fresh cool greens on the side.

TOMATO AND BASIL SALAD

This dish "happened" one day at lunchtime. When I was working on *The New Seasoning* (also published by Simon and Schuster), Ann Collier, my food researcher, came in with a comment that there just wasn't anything in the icebox. So she "sloshed up" this little salad. It is wonderful—and it was all hers! Now it's yours.

5 tomatoes	*freshly ground pepper*
1 tsp. basil	*salt*
6 tbsp. plain yogurt	*Romaine lettuce*
	4 ripe olives

PREPARATION

1. Choose 4 blemish-free tomatoes and leaving the skin on, make a basket out of each. Scoop out the tomato leaving the shell. Make the basket edges jagged.

2. Skin and finely dice the fifth tomato along with the scooped-out parts of the other 4. Mix tomato dicings with the yogurt, pepper and basil.

3. Salt and pepper the inside of the tomatoes. Cut the lettuce to make 2 "leaves" per tomato. Peel the edible part away from the olive seeds, making 3 segments per olive.

4. To assemble: place 2 lettuce "leaves" halfway inside each tomato; spoon mixture into the tomatoes. Add the finishing touch of 3 olive segments per tomato for garnish. Serve on a lettuce leaf. Serves 4.

NUTRITION PROFILE

	CALORIES	PROTEIN	FAT	CARBOHYDRATE
5 tomatoes	200	10 gm.		45 gm.
6 tbsp. yogurt	42	3 gm.	1 gm.	4 gm.
4 ripe olives	18		1.9 gm.	0.3 gm.
	260			

One serving has 65 calories.

TOMATOES IN VINAIGRETTE
WITH WATERCRESS

Fresh from the rigors of a hard, stale day, through a shower and into clean clothes one stumbles to the table. A great need to be refreshed, to have one's digestion brought alive, not absorbed by cream soups, fatty pâté or "egged" salads rustling with croutons. We find the simple sliced tomato and chilled watercress work wonders.

Tomatoes (¼ lb. per person)   1 tsp. basil
Oil   Watercress
Vinegar

PREPARATION

Skin and slice the tomatoes into ¼-inch-thick rings. Lay them flat and overlapping on an oval serving dish and float the dressing (2 parts vinegar to 1 part oil) on top. Add 1 tsp. basil and cover with a plastic film. Place in the refrigerator for at least 4 hours (24 hours will not spoil them). Then drain off the dressing and use that to toss fresh, chilled and picked-over watercress. Serve the two together.

NUTRITIONAL PROFILE

	CALO-RIES	PRO-TEIN	SATU-RATED FAT	CARBO-HYDRATE
4 oz. tomato	22	2 gm.		9 gm.
1 oz. dressing	86		9 gm.	2 gm.
2 oz. watercress	12	0.6 gm.	0.1 gm.	2 gm.
	120			

WINTER SALAD

Even though salad makings are available year round, we feel it's a neat idea to serve a special salad in the winter when snow is about.

This is a splendid contribution that you may find equally suited to hot days. It's rather high in calories but it's all good stuff and it's variety! The yogurt really brings out the flavor of the fruits and the carrots.

3 apples, grated (9–10 oz.)
lemon juice
2 carrots, grated (4 oz.)
½ c. chopped almonds
⅓ c. dried apricots, chopped
  (2 oz.)

⅓ c. pitted dates, chopped
  (2 oz.)
⅓ c. raisins
½ c. yogurt

PREPARATION

1. Grate apples (don't cut) and cover with lemon juice; grate carrots, chop almonds, apricots, and dates. (Dates cut better if knife is dipped in flour before every second or third cut.) Measure out raisins and yogurt.

2. Combine all ingredients in a large bowl. Serve immediately or chill before serving—delicious either way! Serves 8.

NUTRITION PROFILE

	CALO-RIES	PRO-TEIN	FAT	CARBO-HYDRATE
3 apples	210			54 gm.
2 carrots	40	2 gm.		10 gm.
½ c. almonds	425	13 gm.	38.5 gm.	14 gm.
⅓ c. raisins	160	1 gm.		43 gm.
⅓ c. apricots	130	2 gm.		33 gm.
⅓ c. dates	163	1 gm.		43 gm.
½ c. yogurt	42	2 gm.	1 gm.	4 gm.
	1170			

Serves 8 at 146 calories per serving.

Soups

CHICKEN AND BARLEY SOUP

It is still possible to make four servings of soup for under $1.

What is better still, this soup costs about 67¢ or 8¢ a serving and it is delicious—the calorie value is only 62 per serving, so it could be useful for more than economy alone.

8 c. water	*¼ tsp. sage*
1½–2 lbs. chicken backs and	*⅛ tsp. marjoram*
necks	*⅛ tsp. rosemary*
1 tsp. black pepper	*¼ c. barley*
1 tbsp. salt	*2 oz. thinly sliced celery*
¼ tsp. thyme	*2 oz. diced onion*

PREPARATION

1. Measure all ingredients. Chop celery and onion. Rinse chicken parts.

2. Combine all ingredients except celery and cook for 1 hour slowly, with the lid on.

3. Cool and skim fat from the surface. Remove meat from the chicken backs and necks. Separate skin from the meat, discard skin, add meat to the broth (we obtained 7 oz. meat from 1.73 lbs. of backs). Reheat and add celery at the end. Serve immediately. Serves 8.

Time to prepare: 1 hour cooking time and 10 minutes pre-preparation.

NUTRITION AND COST PROFILE

	CALO-RIES	PRO-TEIN	FAT	CARBO-HYDRATE
7 oz. chicken	230	40 gm.	2 gm.	
8 c. broth	56	16 gm.	4 gm.	66 gm.
¼ c. barley	170	4 gm.	1 gm.	36 gm.
2 oz. celery	4			1.5 gm.
2 oz. onion	40	2 gm.		10 gm.
	500			

The number of calories per serving is 62.5. Total cost is 67¢ or 8¢ per serving.

GAZPACHO

No summer soup deserves so widespread a reputation for excellence as this simple recipe. Certainly, the fine dice you have to cut is a tedious business but oh, the colorful, wonderful result! The standard soup can be 96.6 calories per serving *but* we have added a list of extras that can increase the protein to remarkable levels and do great things to vary the soup's flavor.

2 lbs. ripe tomatoes
  (2 pts. canned)
2 oz. black olives
1 oz. spring onion tops
2 oz. green pepper
6–8 oz. cucumber
1 tbsp. fresh parsley
3 oz. radishes (optional)
2 tbsp. lemon juice
2 oz. (¼ c.) red grape juice
2 tbsp. rice vinegar

2 tbsp. olive oil
1 tbsp. strong cold tea
1 c. concentrated gelatinous
  chicken stock
¼ tsp. basil
¼ tsp. tarragon
1 tsp. paprika
1 tsp. salt
pepper to taste
1 clove garlic, crushed

FIRST PREPARE

Skin tomatoes. Finely dice olives, onion tops, green pepper, cucumber, fresh parsley, radishes. Squeeze lemon juice, measure grape juice, vinegar, olive oil, tea, chicken stock, and herbs.

NOW COMBINE

1. Rub large bowl with the crushed garlic clove.
2. Place tomatoes in a blender and blend for 10–15 seconds until well chopped.
3. Pour tomatoes into the bowl, season with basil and tarragon (rubbed between the palms of the hands to bring out the flavor).
4. Add paprika, parsley, chopped vegetables and all other ingredients.
5. Stir to blend. Chill for at least 2 hours before serving. Makes 7 cups.

NUTRITION PROFILE

	WEIGHT	CALO-RIES	PRO-TEIN	FAT	CARBO-HYDRATE
2 lbs. tomatoes	940 gm.	188	9.4 gm.		42.3 gm.
2 oz. black olives	60 gm.	90		12 gm.	
1 oz. onion tops	28 gm.	15	1 gm.		4 gm.
2 oz. green pepper	56 gm.	12			3 gm.
6 oz. cucumber	207 gm.	30	1 gm.		7 gm.
3 oz. radishes	90 gm.	10			2 gm.
1 c. chicken stock	240 gm.	30	5 gm.		3 gm.
2 tbsp. lemon juice	55 gm.	10	0.5 gm.		3 gm.
2 tbsp. vinegar	30 mg.				2 gm.
2 tbsp. olive oil	28 gm.	250		28 gm.	
2 oz. red grape juice	63 gm.	41			10 gm.
		676			

Serves 7 at 96.6 calories per serving.

ONION SOUP

Of all my tests, this turned up the most dramatically different recipe ideas. Essentially it came down to frank opposition on quantity. *Larousse Gastronomique* and *Cordon Bleu* suggest ½ lb. onions to 4 cups of stock, whereas Mme. Benoît of Canada and Michael Field say 2 lbs. (4 *times* as much).

We found 2 lb. to be correct and ½ lb. like dishwater.

Then, on the subject of whether to brown or not to brown these onions, Larousse and Benoît say *no*, Cordon Blue says *lightly brown* and Field says *brown deeply*. We agree with Field.

All sources use butter. I disagree and used sesame/safflower oil. All sources used flour; I used arrowroot.

The result is, without the usual cheese and bread on top, quite good. We look upon the topping as an *extreme burden*.

1 French loaf (1 lb.) = 1315 calories = 82 calories a slice (16 to a loaf).

1 oz. Parmesan cheese = 130 calories (130 + 82 = *212 calories for topping alone!*)

After all that—here is our recipe!

2 lb. peeled onions	2 tsp. naturally brewed soy sauce
1 tbsp. sesame/safflower oil	1 tbsp. arrowroot (optional)
1 qt. (4 c.) Pressure Beef Stock	parsley
page 114	Parmesan cheese, freshly grated

PREPARATION

1. Peel onions and weigh when peeled to make 2 lbs.
2. Cut one onion into neat ¼-inch-thick rings to be used later as a garnish.
3. Finely slice the remainder and shallow fry in the sesame/safflower oil over medium-high heat for 15 minutes until well browned.
4. Pour on the Pressure Beef Stock. Bring to a boil and reduce to a simmer. Add fresh onion rings and continue to cook gently until they are just cooked.
5. Add the soy sauce. Taste and add pepper if you wish. Thicken with arrowroot mixed with a little water, if necessary.

6. Dust with fresh parsley and a very little freshly grated Parmesan if you wish (1 tsp. = 13 calories).

7. Serve very hot and please stay away from the bread rolls!

NUTRITION PROFILE

onion	100 calories
stock	30 calories
oil	32 calories
arrowroot	7 calories
	169 calories

Serves 8 at 42 calories per serving.

SOUPE AU PISTOU

Use this soup as a vehicle for extending your own creativity into a protein explosion. Frankly the writing is on the wall about high-priced meat, and as Christians I feel we should begin to understand how to make do when forced out of the luxury market completely!

1 carrot (2 oz.)
1 small leek (2–3 oz.)
1 stick celery (1 oz.)
4 oz. fresh green beans
1 small zucchini (3 oz.)
1 small potato (2 oz.)
2 medium, fresh tomatoes
(11 oz.)
4 oz. fresh asparagus stalks
½ green pepper (1–2 oz.)
1 large clove garlic

2 tbsp. fresh parsley
3 oz. sharp cheddar cheese
1 14-oz. can red kidney beans
2 tbsp. olive oil
48 oz. cold water
½ tsp. dried basil (or 1 tsp.
fresh)
½ tsp. freshly ground black
pepper
1 tbsp. freshly ground salt
4 oz. fine noodles

FIRST PREPARE

Scrape and cube carrot. Wash leek very thoroughly and slice thinly. Slice celery and green beans. Cube zucchini, potato and tomatoes. Finely slice asparagus stalks and dice green pepper into small pieces. Mash garlic, finely chop parsley. Grate cheese. Open the can of beans and measure out the rest of the ingredients.

NOW COOK

1. In a small dutch oven, heat the oil, fry carrot in the oil. Add the can of beans.
2. Add leek, potatoes, green beans, garlic, green pepper and asparagus. Stir well together.
3. Add zucchini and celery. Cook gently for 5 minutes.
4. Add water and seasonings and noodles. Bring to a boil. Cook until vegetables are tender (8–12 minutes). Add tomato cubes and cheese. Pour into heated bowls. Makes 10½ cups.

NUTRITION PROFILE

	CALO-RIES	PRO-TEIN	FAT	CARBO-HYDRATE
2 oz. carrots	23	1 gm.		6 gm.
2 oz. leeks	20	1 gm.		5 gm.
1 oz. celery	4			1.5 gm.
3 oz. zucchini	12	1 gm.		2 gm.
4 oz. green beans	30	2 gm.		7 gm.
2 oz. potatoes	40	1 gm.		9 gm.
11 oz. tomatoes	60	3 gm.		12 gm.
4 oz. noodles	150	6 gm.	1.5 gm.	28 gm.
4 oz. asparagus	24	2 gm.		4 gm.
1½ oz. green pepper	7	1 gm.		2 gm.
3 oz. cheddar cheese	345	21 gm.	27 gm.	3 gm.
14 oz. kidney beans	345	22 gm.	1 gm.	63 gm.
2 tbsp. olive oil	250		28 gm.	
	1310	61 gm.		

Serves 10; 1 c. has 131 calories and 6.1 gm. protein.

Complementary protein sources: whole-wheat bread, kidney beans, cheddar cheese.

POTATO SOUP

Here is a soup that costs only 55¢ to make. It uses very little that the average home doesn't have or couldn't use for many varied dishes. We enjoy it on cold winter nights—especially in the Rocky Mountains!

1 onion, chopped
1 clove garlic, mashed
4 oz. carrot, chopped
4 oz. celery, chopped
16 oz. potato, chopped uniformly
1 stalk and leaves of parsley
½ tbsp. butter

1½ c .water
¼ tsp. thyme
1½ tsp. salt
¼ tsp. pepper
2 c. milk
4 tbsp. Parmesan cheese

PREPARATION

1. Chop onion, garlic, carrot, celery, potato and parsley. Grate cheese and measure remaining ingredients.

2. In a large saucepan, sauté onion, garlic, carrot and celery in ½ tbsp. butter for several minutes until tender.

3. Add water, potatoes, parsley, thyme, salt and pepper and cook for 5 minutes, covered. Add milk and heat until almost boiling. Serve in mugs with 1½ tsp. cheese on top. Makes 6 cups.

NUTRITION AND COST PROFILE

	CALO- RIES	PRO- TEIN	FAT	CARBO- HYDRATE
1 onion	80	4 gm.		10 gm.
4 oz. carrot	40	2 gm.		10 gm.
4 oz. celery	15			6 gm.
16 oz. potatoes	180	6 gm.		42 gm.
½ tbsp. butter	50		6 mg.	
2 c. milk	290	20 gm.	10 gm.	30 gm.
4 tbsp. Parmesan cheese	100	8 gm.	8 gm.	
	755			

Makes 6 c. at 126 calories/c., costing 9¢/c. or 55¢ for entire recipe.

FARMHOUSE VEGETABLE SOUP

This is a rib-sticker that comes out of my "creative" past when Treena and I ran the Royal Ascot Hotel in England.

It, like all the "oldies," has gone through some changes, mainly to reduce the fats and calories. It is still delicious; in fact the yogurt really gives it style.

6 oz. carrots
6 oz. parsnips
3 oz. onions
2 tbsp. safflower oil
1 clove garlic
1 stalk celery (3 in.)
1 tbsp. tomato paste
20 fl. oz. Pressure Beef Stock
   (see page 114)

freshly ground salt to taste
9 black peppercorns
2 bayleaves
4 parsley stalks
3 thyme sprigs or ¼ tsp.
   ground thyme
4 fl. oz. yogurt or buttermilk

FIRST PREPARE

Wash and peel vegetables. Measure stock and yogurt. Tie herbs in a muslin bag. Slice vegetables medium-thin.

NOW COOK

1. Heat oil in a small dutch oven, add vegetables and sauté gently for 4 minutes.

2. Add tomato paste and stir well to obtain a medium-brown carmelizing of the tomato sugars.

3. Add stock and herbs and simmer 20 minutes or until vegetables are tender. Remove herbs and discard them.

4. Place liquid and vegetables in a blender, and blend until smooth. Add yogurt and blend again. Reheat, but do not boil. Season to taste and serve. Serves 4; makes 3¾ cups.

NUTRITION AND COST PROFILE

	WEIGHT	CALO-RIES	PRO-TEIN	FAT	CARBO-HYDRATE
6 oz. carrots	170 gm.	70	3.5 gm.		17 gm.
6 oz. parsnips	170 gm.	115	2 gm.	1 gm.	15 gm.
3 oz. onions	85 gm.	30	1.5 gm.		8 gm.
2 tbsp. oil	28 gm.	250		28 gm.	
20 fl. oz. stock	600 gm.	75	12.5 gm.		7.5 gm.
3-in. piece celery	14 gm.	2			
1 tbsp. tomato paste	15 gm.	15			4 gm.
4 oz. yogurt	122 gm.	60	4 gm.	2 gm.	6.5 gm.
		617			

Recipe serves 4 at 154 calories each; has 6 gm. protein and costs 53¢ total or 13¼ ¢ per serving.

27 ———————————

Vegetables

USING NUTMEG ON VEGETABLES

Nutmeg is native to the Molucca Islands but grows throughout moist tropical climates. We saw nutmeg trees in Dominica and Jamaica. The fruit breaks open and the seed is the spice. The tree bears fruit for over 50 years. The scarlet aril covering the seed is called mace. Sweet, warm and highly spiced, the whole nutmeg is better because it can be grated as needed.

We use it for milk puddings and custards where we use NFDM (nonfat dry milk) because it helps to offset the absence of fat.

We also use it in vegetables, as shown in these two recipes.

CARROTS

julienne cut 2–3 large carrots
    into 4" x ¼" strips
1 tbsp. butter

salt and pepper
½ tsp. sugar
⅛ tsp. freshly grated nutmeg

PREPARATION

1. Blanch carrots 10 minutes. Cool quickly and store in refrigerator until ready to serve.

2. Place butter in frying pan, add carrots and stir-fry to rapidly

heat through. Season with salt, pepper and sugar, and finally with freshly grated nutmeg. Serve immediately.

Serves 4 at 40 calories/serving.

GREEN BEANS

1 lb. fresh green beans, whole
    but with ends removed
1 tbsp. safflower or corn oil
1 clove garlic, crushed

salt and pepper
⅛ tsp. grated nutmeg
1 tbsp. lemon juice

1. Blanch green beans 5–8 minutes, keep bright green and slightly crisp. Cool quickly and store in refrigerator until ready to use.

2. Pour oil in frying pan, add green beans and garlic and toss well to heat through. Add salt and pepper to season and add nutmeg and lemon juice. Toss well and serve.

Serves 4 at 62.5 calories/serving.

NUTRITION PROFILE

	CALO-RIES	PRO-TEIN	FAT	CARBO-HYDRATE
Carrots (2 whole)	60	3 gm.		15 gm.
1 tbsp. butter	100		12 gm.	
	160 = 40 calories per serving			
1 lb. green beans	120	8 gm.		28 gm.
1 tbsp. lemon juice	5			1 gm.
1 tbsp. oil	125		14 gm.	
	250			

One serving has 62.5 calories.

UNMOLDING AN ASPIC

Unmolding an aspic can often be a real pain. We have devised what we think is a really nifty idea. We call it the "rubber plug and hot towel technique"! The idea is to drive a hole in the top center of your mold (it's better to have a friendly repair shop do it for you). Get a small rubber plug from a hardware store and fit it snugly in the bottom.

Fill the mold with your favorite recipe (rinsing first with iced water) and then chill.

To release, all you do is turn the mold upside down on a plate, remove the rubber to release the pressure vacuum and wrap a hot towel about the mold and count to 5. You'll hear it release itself. Perfect—every time.

BRAISED CELERY

Braised celery hearts are a great favorite of ours. They take a long time to cook and they are a fuss, but in my search for a low-calorie, delicious vegetable I found no close competitor.

We suggest you only do this dish if you have a long slow roast to cook and thus can use the oven more effectively.

2 c. Pressure Beef Stock	¼ tsp. oil
(see page 114)	2 tbsp. arrowroot
1 tbsp. tomato paste	1 celery heart

PREPARATION

Make up Pressure Beef Stock. Remove all fat and season properly. Place tomato paste in oil in pan and brown the mixture *thoroughly* over medium heat. Add stock and stir in to color. Thicken with arrowroot and cold water mixed (2 tbsp. arrowroot).

Precook the celery heart (cut 4 inches long and sliced once, in half lengthways). Trim the root end, clean, and place in cold water, raise to the boil and cook for 10 minutes. Drain and place in a shallow baking dish half covered with the thickened stock.

Bake at 325° F. (with the roast) covered for 1 hour and uncovered for the second hour. Baste with the stock occasionally.

Serve the braising liquid as a sauce with the meat.

CAULIFLOWER AND CHEESE

I have always liked cauliflower and cheese, the head smothered in a rich sauce Mornay (cheese sauce) laden with calories and saturated fats. We have now reformed this elegant vegetable and have discovered to our glee a light delicious vegetable with a new flavor—this time you can actually taste the vegetable!

1 head cauliflower
1 tsp. Parmesan cheese, grated
½ c. Cheese Sauce (see below)

Paprika
Parsley

PREPARATION

Clean 1 head of cauliflower, by trimming off the outer leaves and hollowing out the heavy stem: leave whole. Boil covered in water for 10–15 minutes, no longer, just until tender. Pour off water. Cover with Parmesan Cheese Sauce and 1 tsp. grated Parmesan cheese and place under the broiler for 4 minutes until lightly browned. Dust with paprika and parsley.

CHEESE SAUCE

¼ oz. grated Parmesan (1 heaping tbsp.)
¼ cup milk (2%)
½ tsp. arrowroot

Blend together and heat until almost boiling (190° F.), stirring constantly.

NUTRITION PROFILE

		CALORIES	PROTEIN	SATURATED FAT	CARBOHYDRATE	CALCIUM	VITAMIN A
Parmesan (1 tbsp. + 1 tsp.)		33	2.5 gm.	1+ gm.		90 mg.	80 i.u.
Milk (¼ c. 2%)		36.3	2.5 gm.	4 gm.	3.75 gm.	88 mg.	50 i.u.
Arrowroot (½ tsp.)		4.8					
		74.1					

	WEIGHT	CALORIES	PROTEIN	SATURATED FAT	CARBOHYDRATE	POTASSIUM	VITAMIN C
Cauliflower (cleaned & trimmed)	16 oz.	122	12.2 gm.	0.9 gm.	23.6 gm	1338 mg.	354 mg.
Cauliflower (cooked)	3.5 oz.	22	2.3 gm.	0.2 gm.	4.1 gm.	206 mg.	55 mg.

EGGPLANT

We are delighted with this way of fixing eggplant. So often the problem with this bulbous purple vegetable is the way it blackens and becomes bitter. We use the salt press method and coat the strips in tonic water batter. They are a real treat.

1 eggplant, peeled and
   sliced into ⅓-in. strips
2 oz. flour (½ c.)
2 oz. tonic water
2 eggs

pinch of salt
¼ tsp. dill weed
1 lemon
1½ tsp. Parmesan cheese

PREPARATION

1. Eggplant can be prepared in either of 2 ways:
   a. Place slices in salt water for ½–1 hour (1 tbsp. to 1 or 1½ c. water).
   b. Place slices in a bowl, but lightly salt both sides of each slice first, and place something heavy on top for ½–1 hour ahead of time.

Allow to stand for at least 30 minutes. Pour off liquid, rinse very well and pat dry.

2. Prepare tonic water batter 1–2 hours ahead of time and allow to go flat.

3. Beat eggs well. Add flour and rest of the ingredients except the lemon and Parmesan cheese, and beat well until all lumps are gone. Cover and let stand 1–2 hours.

4. Dip dried eggplant in batter and fry in hot oil 2–3 minutes or until lightly brown on both sides. Drain on a paper towel. Sprinkle 1½ tsp. Parmesan cheese on top and serve. A 1-lb. eggplant makes about 20–25 slices. Squeeze lemon on top immediately before serving.

There was no difference in lack of bitterness by both techniques. One must be careful not to use too much salt and to wash all of it off. Coarse (kosher) salt is too strong and does not wash off very well. This dish is expensive in the winter but cheap in the summer.

NUTRITION PROFILE

	CALO-RIES	PRO-TEIN	FAT	CARBO-HYDRATE
1-lb. eggplant	87.5	4.2 gm.	17 gm.	19.6 gm.
2 oz. flour	227.5	6.5 gm.	0.5 gm.	47.5 gm.
2 oz. tonic water	24			
2 eggs	160	12 gm.	6 mg.	
1 tbsp. Parmesan cheese	25	2 gm.	2 gm.	
1 lemon	20			
	544			

At 20 slices per eggplant, 26 calories per slice.

LENTILS

Even before I became a Christian I was fascinated by Esau's "mess of pottage." How could a man be tempted to give up his birthright for a dried grain stew?

As we wanted to look closely at lentils as a good food at low price, we thought it would be fun to look at this famous Biblical dish. Our first efforts were awful until we got nonscriptural and produced a "New Testament" pottage!

"NEW TESTAMENT" POTTAGE

8 oz. lentils
2 cloves garlic (crushed)
1 tbsp. sesame/safflower oil
¼ tsp. cumin
¼ tsp. coriander
2 ham hocks

¼ tsp. celery salt
2 bayleaves
1 qt. water
Nonfat dried milk (to taste)
Parsley
4 oz. onions, chopped

PREPARATION

1. Cover lentils with 2 cups boiling water, cool and drain.
2. Fry garlic with onions in oil. Add cumin and coriander.
3. Add drained lentils, stir in well and add ham hocks and celery salt plus bayleaves. Cover with 1 qt. (4 c.) water and simmer for 2 hours tightly covered.
4. Remove ham hocks. Cut off rind (outer skin) and finely chop meat and put into the lentils.
5. Add nonfat dried milk to taste. This makes a complete protein dish. (For our taste we added ⅓ cup + 1 tbsp. nonfat dried milk powder with 1 cup water.)

NUTRITION AND COST PROFILE

	CALORIES	PROTEIN	FAT	CARBOHYDRATE	CALCIUM	VITAMIN A
Lentils	770	56 gm.	2.5 gm.	136 gm.	180 mg.	135 i.u.

1 lb. lentils (package or bulk) = 49¢.

WHITE LIMA BEANS

Dried lima beans have always impressed me as being super budget food with little gourmet interest. How wrong I was, and how wrong are the "odd" recipes given here and there for their preparation—no wonder they have a poor reputation.

This is how we set about preparing them:

METHOD A

Bring (8 oz.) beans to a boil in 32 fl. oz. water (4 cups). Turn off heat, cover and let stand for at least 2 hours (overnight is OK). Drain and add 1 cup ham stock, 1 clove garlic, 1 medium onion stuck with 4 cloves, 1 bayleaf, ¼ tsp. thyme and 1 5-oz. piece of celery. Cook slowly for 1½ hours.

METHOD B (Pressure Cooker)

Place 8 oz. lima beans in 16 oz. (2 c.) water plus 16 oz. ham stock. Bring to a boil uncovered. Add same seasonings as above. Cover and let pressure rise to 15 psi. Then time 25 minutes, take off heat and let pressure drop naturally (10 minutes). Remove lid and serve with freshly sliced tomatoes and finely shredded raw spinach folded carefully into the steaming broth. Dust with grated cheese for a complete protein.

MUSHROOMS

Mushrooms are regarded as a rich food, but in reality they weigh light for their visual bulk. We compared their volume/value with peas, carrots and tomatoes and discovered some interesting facts (see below).

Cultivated mushrooms do not need peeling. They should be rinsed just before use (wash only those you actually want to use; keep the rest in a brown paper bag in the refrigerator). Trim off the end of the stalk and either keep whole or quarter them with the stalk attached. Large caps can be finely sliced, dressed with lemon juice and a little cayenne and used raw in salads or as a "heat-up" garnish on meat or fish. The quartered stalks and caps are fine just tossed in a little butter with lemon and cayenne added.

VOLUME/WEIGHT/PRICE COMPARISON

	VOLUME	PRICE/POUND	PRICE/1 C.
8 oz. tomatoes	1 c.	69¢	34.5¢
8 oz. carrots	1 c.	35¢	17.5¢
8 oz. mushrooms	1¾ c.	65¢	19 ¢
8 oz. peas	1 c.	53¢	26.5¢

BRAISED ONIONS

Another excellent vegetable, when braised, is the onion. We use exactly the same braise liquid as we do with celery (see page 161), but the vegetable takes more time and is a little more complicated. Once again, it should only be made when the oven is planned to be in use for 1–1½ hours at 325° F.

4 onions, 3 in. in diameter
3 c. water
1 clove garlic, crushed
2 finely chopped mushrooms

2 tsp. sesame/safflower oil
1 tbsp. lemon juice
1–2 slices bacon, uncooked

PREPARATION

Place onions in cold water and bring to the boil, then boil for 20 minutes. Fry the finely chopped mushrooms in the sesame/safflower oil and add the lemon juice. Remove onions from water and take out the centers by cutting off the top and easing the core out with a fork. Chop the center "leaves" finely with the crushed garlic mixed with the fried mushrooms. Place this mixture into the vacated centers of the onions and top each off with a small piece of bacon. Place in a *small* oven-proof baking dish—half cover with braising sauce and bake uncovered at 325° F. for 1½ hours or until tender. Serve the sauce on the side as gravy for a roast.

SPINACH SOUFFLÉ

Soufflés tend to worry some folks, but this one isn't the kind that needs to rear up out of the dish like a status-seeking monster. It is basically a lightened creamed spinach that is easy to fix and earns many compliments.

Go to it with confidence—maybe it will rear up for you?

1 lb. trimmed fresh spinach or
  2 8-oz. packages frozen
  spinach
	Black pepper
	Nutmeg
	Salt

1 tbsp. sesame/safflower oil	3 egg yolks
1 tbsp. arrowroot	4 egg whites
¼ c. whole milk	

PREPARATION

Weigh 1 lb. trimmed spinach or defrost 2 packages (8 oz.) of frozen spinach. Cut off heavy stalks before weighing. Wash fresh spinach well in at least 4 rinse-waters. Place in a heavy-based large saucepan with 1 tbsp. sesame/safflower oil well mixed into the leaves before you start. Cook over medium heat, lid on, for 4 minutes. Stir and toss. Pour off any water in the bottom and remove cooked leaves. Blend until smooth in blender/chopper at medium speed. Pour into a hand sieve and press out all surplus moisture. Retain this juice. Turn chopped spinach into a small saucepan and cook over medium heat to remove the excess moisture. Add the arrowroot and pour back the removed moisture gradually, together with the milk. Season this mix highly with black pepper, nutmeg and with a *touch* of salt. Add the egg yolks, stir in well and let cool on a plate. Beat egg whites very stiff and fold in. Bake in a 7-in. soufflé dish at 400° F. for 20 minutes.

Serve immediately. This can also be sent to the table in individual small dishes.

STIR-FRIED WESTERN VEGETABLES

Stir-fried vegetables are known as a part of Far Eastern cookery. For its *proper* execution you need a *wok* or *wo* (the right spelling) and a special gas fire with large flame jets. It is possible, however, to *borrow* their technique and translate it into our simple skillet and regular range use.

First, the vegetables used should be those we know and can purchase easily and inexpensively, such as brussels sprouts, cauliflower, mushrooms, carrots, celery, scallions, etc. We need some *seasoning* ingredients such as fresh garlic, root ginger and naturally brewed soy sauce.

Cutting the vegetables correctly for quick cooking is vital. We have found that following certain cutting techniques helps to hasten cooking and preserves an attractive finished appearance. The list is given in the order in which the vegetables are to be cooked, from toughness to delicacy, so that an *even* degree of doneness is achieved at the end.

The pan should be large, at least 10″ diameter, and coated with a good oil such as 1 part cold-pressed sesame seed oil mixed with 20 parts safflower oil. 4 tbsp. is usually enough. The pan is then heated over medium-high flame and the foods added in quick succession, stirring all the time with a spatula, fork, or turner.

All the vegetables must be cut and ready *before* you begin to cook.

1. *Garlic* (1 partly crushed clove).

2. *Scallions* (5). Cut off white ends and add them first, keeping green tops for later.

3. *Brussels sprouts* (8). Cut in quarters lengthways.

4. *Celery* (2 sticks). Slice ¼ in. thick diagonally; cut round side up.

5. *Carrots* (2 medium = 4 oz.). Peel and slice diagonally ⅛ in. thick.

6. *Cauliflower* (4 oz.). Tops only; cut into small "flowers" the size of a 25¢ piece.

7. *Mushrooms* (2 oz.). Cut caps into quarters (remove stalks and use for stock).

8. *Ginger root* (¼ tsp.). Freshly grate from fresh (or dried) whole root.

9. *Scallions* (5). Green tops cut into 1-in.-long pieces (see 2, above).

10. *Soy sauce* (1 tbsp.). Add at last moment. Place lid on top, toss well and serve.

Makes enough for 4 vegetable servings or 2 complete dinners.

Caution. This technique can become a stumbling block to those who believe it is the *only* way to cook vegetables. The fact is that it isn't without blame in the list of damaging methods. It exposes cut surfaces to light, heat and air while adding unnecessary fat to a consumption rate already known to be excessive. (Please see page 89 for technical support of this criticism.)

TOMATO IN "NEW WINE" ASPIC

Ice cold and full of tomato, a rich red aspic can set people's appetites on the march on really humid summer days.

We make ours up with:

10 medium/large fresh summer tomatoes (skinned)	2 tbsp. rice vinegar
2 pkg. unflavored gelatin dissolved in 1½ c. water	¼ tsp. ground black pepper
	½ tsp. salt
1 cup red grape juice	1 tsp. basil

PREPARATION

Skin and cut tomatoes into quarters, removing all the seeds but leaving the other flesh (see illustration). Reserve quarters. Reserve inner pulp minus the seeds. Combine gelatin, grape juice, vinegar and spices in a bowl and chill to an egg-white consistency. Chill mold thoroughly in the deep freeze. When gelatin mixture is ready, remove 2-qt. mold from deep freeze and rinse quickly in ice-cold water. Immediately add 1 cup of the gelatin mixture and roll it around the mold to set about ¼ in. thick. Lay the reserved tomato quarters into the mold like leaves overlapping upward to the rim (see illustration).

Combine the reserved inner pulp with the remaining gelatin mixture and add more vinegar or salt according to your taste. Pour into the mold. Set to chill and turn out when thoroughly cold (see page 160 on how to successfully unmold an aspic).

Serve with homemade cottage cheese (Cheese Hangup, page 123) for a good summer meal.

CABBAGE AND ONIONS

Here is an extremely simple and absolutely delicious cabbage recipe.

8 oz. (¼ in.) sliced onion
24 oz. (¼ in.) sliced cabbage
1 tbsp. sesame/safflower oil
¼ tsp. salt

½ tsp. white pepper
1 tsp. dill weed
1 tbsp. parsley, chopped

PREPARATION

1. Slice the onions and the cabbage ¼ in. thick.
2. Gently fry onions in a skillet in the oil. Stir and cook until just softened, but *not* colored.
3. Add the cabbage, salt and pepper, toss together and cover tightly. Cook for 8 minutes over a medium heat, tossing from time to time.
4. When the cabbage is cooked but still crisp, add the dill and

parsley. Taste for other seasonings, toss well and turn into a dish.
Serves 4 huge portions at 50 calories per serving.

NUTRITION PROFILE

	CALO-RIES	PRO-TEIN	FAT	CARBO-HYDRATE
Onions (8 oz.)	30	1.5 gm.		7 gm.
Cabbage (24. oz.)	45	3 gm.		9 gm.
1 tbsp. oil	125		14 gm.	

28

Seafood

BAKED FISH

A 6-lb whole fish makes a splendid meal for 6 people and if fresh is really delicious. If the fish is frozen, we recommend a good soaking in ice-cold salted water for at least an hour after it has been gutted, wiped clean all over and has had the head and tail removed. Remember to scrape off all scales!

PREPARATION

To bake the fish (a 6-lb. fish usually weighs just over 4 lb. when trimmed), place in a baking dish that is deep enough so that the rim is level with the body of the fish when raised on a rack (see below) and viewed sideways.

Season 2 tbsp. sesame/safflower oil with ½ tsp. salt and ½ tsp. white pepper.

Cut fish in slashes diagonally down each flank, about 2 in. apart and ½ in. deep. Rub seasoned oil into the fish, both sides. Lay on a small cake-cooler rack that will fit inside the baking dish. Scatter 1 tbsp. fennel seed into the bottom of the dish. Bake at 350° F. for 15 minutes on each side (see illustrations on page 174 for turning instructions).

When served, strip off all the outer skin—especially if the fish has been deep frozen, as the inside fat may have become rancid.

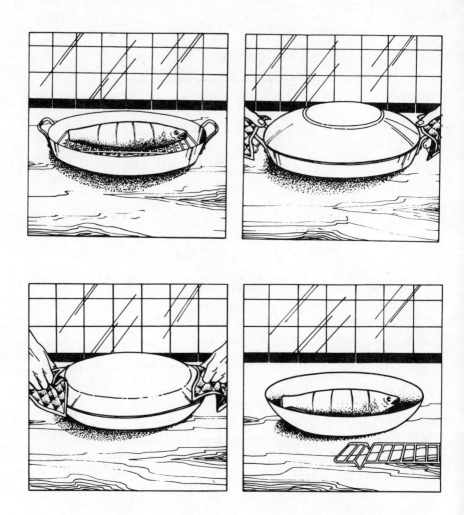

NUTRITION PROFILE

	CALORIES	PROTEIN	FAT
Less than 6½ lb. fish	241	14.3 gm.	19.9 gm.
More than 6½ lb. fish	524	7.9 gm.	54.4 gm.

Please note the tremendous difference in caloric value. This is mainly found immediately below the skin as a heavy fat layer.

DILL WEED FISH SAUCE

The French once said that they had a thousand sauces and one religion, whereas the English appeared to have a thousand religions and only one sauce—and that was parsley! In an effort to undo this slur, we have added another sauce while seriously praying for a reduction in the number of denominations!

fish stock:
14 oz. fish bones (no heads)
1 onion
¼ tsp. thyme
20 oz. water
¼ tsp. salt
¼ tsp. pepper

4 6-oz. fish fillets
1 tsp. soy sauce
1 tbsp. arrowroot
¼ c. milk or light cream
¼ tsp. dill weed

PREPARATION

1. Place left-hand-column ingredients in a saucepan, cover and simmer for 20 minutes.

2. Place fish fillets in a shallow pan such as a frying pan that has a lid. Pour stock through a strainer and measure out 20 oz. (2½ cups). Pour over the fillets in the pan. Cover and poach for 8 minutes, only.

3. Remove fish to a heated plate, cover and keep hot.

4. Cook stock down to 1 c. Mix soy sauce, arrowroot and milk. Remove stock from heat and add most but not all the arrowroot, stirring constantly.

5. Return to the heat and continue stirring. Add the rest of the arrowroot, if needed, but wait until the sauce boils before adding the remainder.

6. Stir in the dill weed at the last minute. Pour over heated fish and serve. Serves 4.

NUTRITION PROFILE

	CALORIES	PROTEIN	FAT	CARBOHYDRATE
20 oz. stock	30			
1 tbsp. arrowroot	29			
¼ c. light cream	106	1.5 gm.	10.3 gm.	2.3 gm.

Makes 1¼ c. sauce at 165 calories or 41 calories per serving.

BAKED FISH IN PAPER PASTRY

Various coatings are used to seal in the moistness in light-flesh foods such as fish and chicken. The bread crumbs or light batters are the obvious ones, but both pick up oil or grease and rather defeat the purpose by adding a snare for the feet of those who would prefer to weigh less. To overcome this, there is an incredible wrapping; it's a vegetable parchment paper obtainable through health food and gourmet stores. The paper is cut away before serving, and the fish is fragrant and full of moisture. (You might use foil, but the cooking temperature will need to be reduced to 400° F. and it's harder to strip off.)

1 small onion
1 clove garlic
½ green pepper (2–3 oz.)
10 oz. fresh tomato flesh
Safflower or corn oil
⅛ tsp. basil

½–1 tsp. freshly ground salt
Freshly ground black pepper
4 sheets vegetable parchment paper
4 servings 6-oz. fresh fish fillets such as ocean perch

PREPARATION

1. Very finely chop the first 4 ingredients.
2. Sauté them lightly in 1 tbsp oil. Add the basil, salt and pepper, stir to mix and remove from the heat.
3. Cut 4 circles, each 12 in. across, from the vegetable parchment paper. Lightly oil the inside of each paper.
4. Place one 6-oz. fillet in each piece of paper. Scoop 1–2 tbsp. of

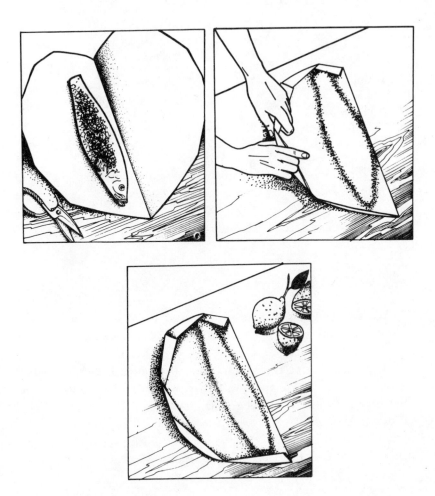

the sautéed mixture on top of the fish. Fold the paper in half and tightly fold around the edges to seal the food inside.

5. Lightly oil the paper on both sides outside. Bake on a cookie sheet for 5 minutes at 475° F. Watch the paper constantly so that it doesn't burn. (The fish will be done in this time if filling is spread out in one layer and the fillets are fairly thin.)

6. Remove from the oven and serve immediately. Serves 4.

NUTRITION AND COST PROFILE

	CALORIES	PROTEIN	FAT	CARBOHYDRATE
1 onion	40	2 gm.		10 gm.
½ green pepper	7.5	0.5 gm.		2 gm.
10 oz. tomato	64	3 gm.	0.6 gm.	14 gm.
2 tbsp. oil	250		28 gm.	
24 oz. perch	826	135 gm.	28 gm.	
	1187.5			

Four portions are 297 calories per serving. One 6-oz. portion of breaded and fried ocean perch is 390 calories (saving 97 calories per serving).

One lb. ocean perch fillets costs $1.19.

RAW FISH IN QUICK PICKLE

We first had this dish when we lived in New Zealand. It is a favorite in Tahiti, where one version is called *Poisson Cru* and is laced with coconut cream before serving.

This recipe turns the concept into a distinguished "tuna salad" alternative. We suggest you await your guests' inquiries and respond after they have eaten! By then your guests may be persuaded to try making it themselves.

Perfectly fresh fish is the key to this dish. We believe, after comparing the two, that frozen fish does not work.

Fresh fish (not frozen)
Onions
Lemons
2 oz. each diced carrots, celery
and cucumber for each
pound of fish

⅞ c. Blender Mayonnaise
for each pound of fish
(see page 143)
lettuce leaves

PREPARATION

The fish is boned, skinned and cut into ½-inch pieces. For each 1 lb. of chopped fish add 4 oz. onion cut into fine rings. Mix these rings with the fish and add the juice of 4 lemons.

Set this simple pickle to mature in a covered glass bowl or jar for at least 8 hours (we have left it for 24 hours without harm).

The flesh will now be white. Drain, throw out onions and lemon juice and add finely diced (¼ in.) carrots, celery and cucumber. Combine this salad with our Blender Mayonnaise. Serve well chilled on lettuce leaves.

SHRIMP SALAD

Choux pastry shells may be found in many recipe books or they can be purchased boxed by the two dozen at good bakeries. We recommend the 1–1½-in. diameter "mouth size" for this dish.

The dish is served cold as an appetizer before sitting down to a party dinner or as a covered dish at a buffet evening. At less than 30 calories each, the stuffed choux are a delicious, nourishing alternative to many dangerously fattening starters.

8 oz. cooked medium shrimp	*1 tbsp. capers*
⅓ c. cider vinegar	*Dash of Tabasco sauce*
4 oz. mung bean sprouts	*⅓ c. Blender Mayonnaise*
½ tsp. dill weed	*(see page 143)*

FIRST PREPARE

Steam shrimp in ⅓ c. water and ⅓ c. cider vinegar for 10 minutes or until all shrimp are very red. Drain and remove the shell and veins. (Be sure to start with 1 lb. raw in order to have enough). Cut shrimp in long threads (1 in. × ¼ in.). Weigh out bean sprouts. (Bean sprouts may need to be cut in half, if they are too long.) Measure out dill weed and capers. Prepare Blender Mayonnaise and measure out ⅓ cup.

NOW COMBINE

Combine all ingredients and fill shells, or refrigerate and let the flavors mingle before serving. Makes 2–2½ cups. 1 level tbsp. is enough to fill the shells. Fills 38 small choux pastry shells.

NUTRITION PROFILE

	CALORIES	PROTEIN	FAT	CARBOHYDRATE
8 oz. shrimp	266	56 gm.	2.6 gm.	2.6 gm.
4 oz. mung beans	45.5	5 gm.	0.26 gm.	8.6 gm.
⅓ c. Blender Mayonnaise	342	1 gm.	66 gm.	
	653.5			

This amount fills 38 small choux pastry shells for 17 calories each. Mung beans are a good source of vitamin K and of the B vitamins.

STEAMED SHRIMP

I must insist that precooked shrimp are tasteless; in fact, they just look the part. Better by far to buy them raw and frozen ("green") and steam them yourself.

Here is a simple recipe. Remember, shrimp are a good source of protein with very little fat.

1 lb. raw shrimp, medium
4 spring onions
2 cloves garlic, crushed
2 stalks parsley
¼ c. rice vinegar

¼ c. water
2 bayleaves
Peel from ¼ orange and ¼ lemon
1 tbsp. fennel seed

PREPARATION

1. Keep shrimp frozen until ready to use. Prepare or otherwise measure out all ingredients.

2. Put vinegar and water in the bottom of a large saucepan. Place all other ingredients except the shrimp in the liquid after it has been brought to a boil.

3. Place a metal vegetable steamer over the hot liquid and put the shrimp in the steamer. Cover tightly and steam for 10 minutes.

4. Serve hot or cold, but remove shrimp from steamer after cooking or they become too strongly seasoned. Serves 4.

NUTRITION PROFILE

	CALO-RIES	PRO-TEIN	FAT	CARBO-HYDRATE	CAL-CIUM	IRON	VITA-MIN A
1 lb. shrimp	500	105 gm.	5 gm.	5 gm.	490 mg.	13 mg.	250 i.u.

29

Rice

CUMIN RICE

We wanted to create a mild but aromatic rice dish that could be laced with bits and pieces of meat, poultry or fish leftovers and make a democratic backdrop for them all. We found that cumin answered our need. Its delicacy reminds one of curry, without curry's heat.

⅔ c. long-grain rice
1 c. water
2 tsp. ground cumin
1 tbsp. oil

2 tbsp. slivered almonds
4 tbsp. plumped raisins
Freshly ground salt and
    pepper to taste

PREPARATION

1. Measure all ingredients. Plump raisins as follows: place in a small saucepan with ½ c. water, bring to a boil, remove from heat and allow to sit for 15–20 minutes.

2. Boil the rice gently in ½ c. water together with the cumin and a dash of salt for 10 minutes. Then put the rice in a colander and return to the same pot, cover and steam over the lowest heat for 5 more minutes.

3. Place 1 tbsp. oil in a frying pan, add the rice, almonds, raisins, and salt and pepper to taste. Stir to warm the rice and mix the ingredients. Serve immediately. Serves 4.

NUTRITION PROFILE

	CALO-RIES	PRO-TEIN	FAT	CARBO-HYDRATE
⅔ c. rice	372	4 gm.		92 gm.
1 tbsp. oil	125		14 gm.	
2 tbsp. almonds	106	3.2 gm.	9.6 gm.	3.4 gm.
4 tbsp. raisins	80			22 gm.
	683			

Serves 4 at 171 calories/serving.

PARMESAN RICE CRUST
FOR SPINACH QUICHE

Would you be interested in a pie crust that used, instead of the regular flour, fat and water, a combination of rice, egg, soy sauce and Parmesan cheese?

The idea fascinated us and after some trial and much error, this technique evolved. It is actually quite easy, delicious, slightly less fattening than pie crust but more expensive. The spinach filling can be used with your regular pie crust.

PARMESAN RICE CRUST

⅔ c. long-grain rice
½ tsp. salt
1 beaten egg white

1 tsp. soy sauce
¼ c. grated Parmesan cheese
pepper to taste

PREPARATION

1. Cook rice 20 minutes in 1½ cups of water.
2. After the rice is cooked, mix the egg white, soy sauce, cheese and pepper and add to the rice. Stir well to mix and press into a 9-in. pie pan. Bake at 375° F. for 25–30 minutes until it begins to get crusty and dries out.

SPINACH SOUFFLÉ FILLING

1 lb. trimmed spinach	*Black pepper*
1 tbsp. sesame/safflower oil	*Trace of salt*
1 tbsp. arrowroot	*3 egg yolks*
¼ c. whole milk	*4 egg whites*
Nutmeg, grated	*4 oz. Swiss cheese*

PREPARATION

1. Weigh 1 lb. trimmed spinach (or defrost 2 8-oz. frozen packages). Cut off heavy stalks before weighing. Wash well in at least 4 washings.

2. Place spinach in a heavy-based *large* saucepan with 1 tbsp. oil well mixed into the leaves before you start. Cook over a medium heat for 4 minutes. Stir and toss. Pour off any excess water in the bottom and remove cooked leaves.

3. Place spinach in blender and blend until smooth. Pour into a hand sieve and press out all surplus moisture. Add arrowroot and add back the removed moisture gradually, together with the milk.

4. Season this mixture highly with pepper, nutmeg and a trace of salt. Add 3 egg yolks, stir in well and let cool on a plate. Fold in 4 stiffly beaten egg whites.

5. Place spinach filling into rice crust. On the top of the pie make a lattice work of Swiss cheese (4 oz.) using very thin slices ¼–½ in. wide. Bake at 400° F. for 20 minutes. Serves 6.

NUTRITION PROFILE

	CALORIES
⅔ c. rice	372
1 egg white	15
¼ c. Parmesan cheese	165
	552

Spinach soufflé has 770 calories total.

This serves 2 as a main dish at 660 calories per serving.

The pie crust has 92 calories per serving (6).

1 slice of quiche has 220 calories (6).

Complementary protein sources are rice + milk product + egg white.

FRIED RICE

Chinese Fried Rice is an excellent vehicle for stretching one pork chop to feed three or four people. It weighs heavy in the caloric scales but it's easy and most fragant and attractive. Just compare the figures for a sirloin steak at the end of the recipe and think about your protein needs!

1 10 oz. pork chop, loin cut
2½ oz. green pepper
  (½ pepper)
1 oz. green onion tops (4)
2 oz. radishes (4–6)
1 tbsp. pork grease

1 clove garlic
2 tsp. soy sauce
¼ tsp. fresh gingerroot
15 oz. red kidney beans (1 can)
2 c. cooked, dry long-grain rice

PREPARATION

1. Cook rice only 8 minutes and spread out to steam cold. Vegetable pieces must be cut very small and symmetrically.

2. Remove excess fat from pork chop. Chop green onion tops and cut radishes into eighths; thinly slice green pepper; measure out remaining ingredients.

3. Gently fry pork chop until done (keep moist). Remove meat from pan, cut into small pieces, discard bone and fat.

4. Leave 1 tbsp. grease in skillet. Add garlic, soy sauce, and gingerroot. Brown green onions and pepper, add radishes, meat, rice and beans. Heat through and serve immediately. Serves 4.

NUTRITION PROFILE

	CALO-RIES	PRO-TEIN	FAT	CARBO-HYDRATE
2 oz. radishes	5			1 gm.
2 c. rice	450	8 gm.		100 gm.
2 c. kidney beans	460	30 gm.	2 gm.	84 gm.
5½ oz. pork chop meat	420	48.4 gm.	22.6 gm.	
1 tbsp. grease	115		13 gm.	
2½ oz. green pepper	7.5	0.5 gm.		2 gm.
1 oz. onion tops	10	0.5 gm		
	1467.5			

This is an inexpensive protein dish with pork chop, rice and kidney beans as protein sources. Total protein is 87.4 gm. Serves 4 with 21.9 gm. usable protein each. (1 3-oz. sirloin steak has 20 gm. protein.) One serving has 367 calories.

	CALO-RIES	PRO-TEIN	FAT	COST
Fried Rice	367	22 gm.	9.4 gm.	42¢
3-oz. sirloin	330	20 gm.	27 gm.	45¢ (boneless)
				39¢ (bone-in)

(Most people have at least 6 oz. of steak.)

30

Pastry and Bread

QUICK YEAST BREAD INGREDIENTS

If you have never attempted to make bread in any form may we introduce you now to this wonderfully satisfying art? We have set it up in three steps.

1. Knowing the ingredients and what they do.
2. How to mix.
3. How to mold, in this case bread rolls.

Firstly, you will need:

Flour. All-purpose flour is fine—you can add various other flours at a 1 to 4 ratio (i.e., 1 c. whole wheat to 3 c. all purpose). All-purpose flour is needed for proper rising.

Oil. 2 oz. (¼ c.) safflower oil for each 4 c. flour. Acts as a keeper

by making a batch moist. You can do without, but bread goes stale very rapidly (after 1 day's time).

Yeast. ¼ oz. (7 g. or ¾ tbsp.) per package. Should support 3–4 c. flour (4 c. means longer prove time).

Sugar. Feeds the yeast. Yeast has to grow on some food, and it does well on sugar, honey or molasses, but sugar is easiest (1 tsp. to 4 c. flour).

Liquid. 50/50 milk and water ratio (1 c. liquid to 4 c. flour) or potato water or rice water can be used and the salt and sugar eliminated as the *starch water* satisfies both needs. Milk plus flour greatly increases the protein value of the bread, compared to water alone with flour.

MIXING A BASIC BREAD DOUGH

To mix bread dough, the conditions must be *perfect*.

1. All the utensils should be clean and warm.

2. Measure flour *unsifted* if using a cup measure, but we recommend a pair of scales and accurately weighed ingredients. There is a difference! For convenience we do use cups here.

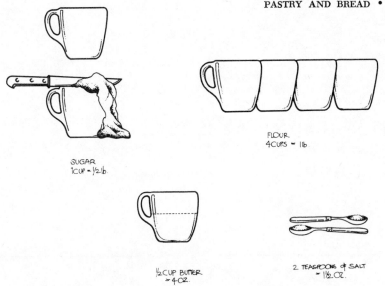

SUGAR
1 CUP = ½ lb.

FLOUR
4 CUPS = 1 lb

½ CUP BUTTER
= 4 OZ.

2 TEASPOONS of SALT
= 1½ OZ.

3. Liquid must be at about 100°–110° F. For this you need a simple thermometer from any hardware store for about $4. Consider your time at $2.00 per hour and the waste plus food cost just due to the milk factor!

4. Sprinkle yeast with sugar or honey over warmed liquid and oil. Let it sit 5 minutes, then combine *well*. Pour yeast mixture into a well of flour and stir in thoroughly. Knead well for 5 to 10 minutes—place into a greased bowl, grease top by turning in the bowl, cover with a cloth and set in a 140° F. oven and turn off the heat. Prove for 30 minutes or until doubled in size.

KNOCKING BACK A BREAD DOUGH AND MAKING ROLLS

Take completed, proved dough from oven. Punch in the center and turn out onto a board. Knead again lightly. Cut into 1-oz. pieces and shape into rolls. Place onto a "bright" sheet (aluminum), well greased (use light oil). Cover & allow to rise 30 minutes.

Place into 375° F. preheated oven for 12–15 minutes to bake.

Turn out onto a cake rack to cool.

Brush with egg white or melted butter before baking to give a glaze.

KNOCKING BACK A BREAD DOUGH

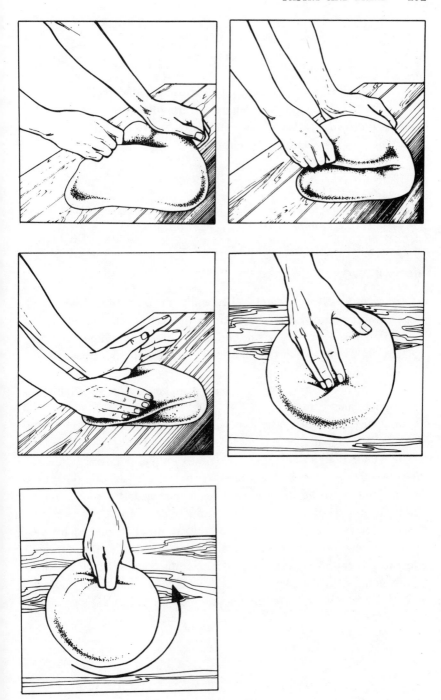

EGG BRAIDS

A "fancy loaf" is one that employs a complicated recipe or form. This is a simple recipe with an easy form that winds up looking fantastically complicated—so in many ways it fits our bill; a kind of maximum return for a minimum effort!

8 c. flour	1 tbsp. salt
½ c. butter or oil	4 tbsp. sugar (¼ c.)
2 eggs plus 1 egg white	2 packages yeast or 2 tbsp.
2 c. reconstituted nonfat	(from jar)
dried milk	

PREPARATION

1. Measure all ingredients. Heat milk and butter to 115–120° F. Place yeast in warmed liquid and stir well. Allow to sit 5 minutes.

2. Mix 6 c. flour, salt, sugar, and yeast/liquid ingredients.

3. Add 2 eggs and mix well. Stir in enough flour so it doesn't stick (1½–2 c.).

4. Turn out onto a floured board and knead for 8–10 minutes, until smooth and satiny.

5. Place dough in a clean, greased bowl and grease the top of the dough. Cover and allow dough to double in size (1 hour).

6. Punch dough down and divide into 4 equal portions. Roll each piece to a 24–30-in. rope. Then braid each 2 pieces, starting out in an "X" position, with the top piece going to the top left. Bring it down under the top right one, then over and under until it is used up. Continue each arm going back to the uppermost right one each time.

7. Place 2 braided loaves on a greased cookie sheet, cover and allow to rise for 45 minutes to 1 hour or until double. Brush loaf just before going into the oven with a raw, beaten egg white. Bake at 375° F. for 20 minutes. Cool immediately on a cake rack.

NUTRITION AND COST PROFILE

	CALORIES	PROTEIN	FAT	CARBOHYDRATE	
8 c. flour	3640	104 gm.		760	gm.
3 eggs	240	18 gm.	6 gm.		
½ c. butter	810	1 gm.	51 gm.	1	gm.
2 c. nonfat dried milk, prepared	180	18 gm.		24	gm.
¼ c. sugar	192.5			99.5	gm.
2 packages yeast	40	6 gm.		6	gm.
	5102.5				

This recipe makes 2 2-lb. loaves at a cost of 56¢ per loaf. It will keep well up to 1 week and it freezes beautifully. You can get at least 20 large slices per loaf, but we recommend cutting each slice in half (a whole slice is very large). Therefore, ½ slice is 64 calories.

FIVE-MINUTE
FLAKY PASTRY PIE TOP

A really good, full-of-flavor, crusty pie top is almost *the* perfect topping for a meaty stew. But so often the crust is sodden, pallid, chewy and worst of all perhaps, riddled with calories owing much to saturated fats.

We made up a pastry that needs *speed*, always works and uses only 4 oz. of polyunsaturated safflower oil to a 1 lb. 8 oz. mix which is usually sufficient for a top crust for 12 people (at 220 calories).

If you look at any good French-style cookbook you'll see that a puff pastry uses 3¾ c. flour (454 g.) = 1659 calories, 1 lb. butter (454 gm.) = 3240 calories, 2 egg yolks = 120 calories and 8 fl. oz. water = 5019 calories for 2 lbs. 9 oz. pastry. Ounce for ounce, this gives us: Safflower oil pastry = 110.5 calories per oz., puff pastry = 122.8 calories per oz.—and the latter is all saturated fats.

So, if you also want to make a top crust in 5 minutes instead of taking at least 1 hour, join us with this easy idea.

MAKING ROLLS

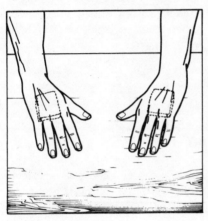

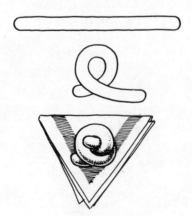

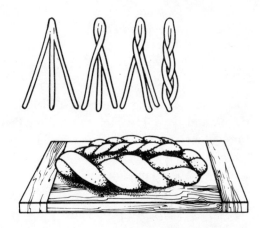

MAKING
FLAKY PASTRY

4 oz. (½ c.) safflower oil　　　　*½ c. ice water*
1 lb. all-purpose flour (4 c.　　　 *Pinch of salt*
　sifted)

PREPARATION

Measure all ingredients first. Mix salt and sifted flour, then add
the oil and *shake the bowl* to combine flour and oil. Stir in water and
turn out on a floured board to knead lightly and quickly. Roll out *twice,*
wrap in waxed paper and cool before use. Roll out thin and add to an
already prepared mixture.

THE PUT-ON PIE TOP

The pie crust probably started out as a sealing device to keep
long-cooking meat completely covered. Pies are still made in this
manner, but more frequently they are made by cooking the filling in a
pressure cooker or casserole or even a slow cooker and then placing
the mix in a pie dish, covering with a flaky pastry and baking at a
high temperature (450° F.) for 25 minutes.

I believe this is the best way to eliminate the sodden crust that
absorbs the natural fatty surface of any meat stew. The secret is to be
sure that the stew is fat skimmed and fully seasoned and garnished
before the top goes on.

As for the top, use the safflower oil Flaky Pastry (see page 193)
and roll it out, folding as illustrated 4 times. After the last rolling out,
let relax for 5 minutes, cut a thick strip and lay it on the pie plate rim,
secured with water. Then brush with water and roll on the pastry.

Trim and pinch the edges, brush with an egg wash, cut steam
holes and bake.

NEWFOUNDLAND PIZZA TEACAKE

I frankly admit to being the author of this gastronomic pun. You
may not receive my humor too well, but the "biggest bun in the
business" will receive many compliments.

Try it and see, especially when it's cold enough to justify the
nearly 200-calorie buttered snack!

2 oz. (¼ c.) butter or oil
1½ lbs. (6 c.) flour
12 oz. nonfat dried milk,
   reconstituted
1 egg
2 tbsp. sugar

6 oz. currants and raisins
1 oz. each lemon and orange
   peel
2 tbsp. (2 packages) dry yeast
1 tbsp. salt

PREPARATION

1. Measure all ingredients. Cut up peels and weigh out. Mix 3 c. flour with the sugar and salt. Heat milk and shortening to 115° F. Add dry yeast, stir well to mix and let sit for 5 minutes.

2. Pour warm liquid into dry ingredients, add egg and blend very well. Stir in the fruit and peel. Add the rest of the flour, 1 c. at a time. Stir and then mix well with the hands between additions.

3. When dough becomes stiff, turn out onto a well-floured board and knead 8–10 minutes until smooth and satiny. Place dough in a greased bowl and grease the top. Cover with a clean tea towel and allow to rise 1 hour or until double in size.

4. Punch dough down and mold it into a greased pizza pan. Brush top with egg white. Allow to double again and bake at 375° F. for 20 minutes or until a deep golden brown. Remove bread from pan immediately and cool on a cake rack. To serve, split bread horizontally, butter each half and place under the broiler for 5 minutes or less to toast lightly and melt the butter.

NUTRITION PROFILE

	CALO-RIES	PRO-TEIN	FAT	CARBO-HYDRATE
2 oz. oil	500		56 gm.	
6 c. flour	2730	78 gm.	6 gm.	570 gm.
12 oz. nonfat dried milk, reconstituted	61	6 gm.		9 gm.
1 egg	80	6 gm.	6 gm.	
2 tbsp. sugar	80			22 gm.
6 oz. currants	480			132 gm.
2 oz. peel	180			46 gm.
2 tbsp. yeast	40	6 gm.		6 gm.

This will serve 24 at 173 calories per serving (without butter). (1 tsp. butter has 33.3 calories.)

MIDDLE EASTERN POCKET BREAD

Some good supermarkets now stock this bread. It makes a great sandwich. All you do is slide the filling into the round bread "pocket" and munch!

Some interested cooks with baking skills may want to try this recipe for themselves. It was one of the early Holy Breads for Holy Communion.

9 c. unbleached flour	3 c. potato water
1½ tbsp. (2 packages) yeast	¼ c. sugar
1 tsp. salt	(No oil)

PREPARATION

1. In a large bowl measure out 3½ c. flour. Mix salt, sugar and instant yeast with the flour. (If yeast is not instant, dissolve yeast first in ½ c. warm, not hot, potato water and stir into the dry ingredients.)

2. Heat potato water to 115–125° F. Pour water into the center of the flour and mix with a spoon.

3. Gradually add the rest of the flour, ½ c. at a time.

4. Turn dough out onto a floured board and knead 8–10 minutes until smooth and satiny.

5. Place dough in a greased bowl and grease top of dough. Cover and let rise again.

6. Divide dough into small lemon-sized pieces. Roll out *very* flat (¼ in. or less). Place on ungreased cookie sheets and bake at 475° F. for 7 minutes. (To brown, put under the broiler 1–2 minutes later on.) Makes 20–25 flat loaves with a pocket. (They puff up when they bake, but go flat as they cool. This is normal.)

NUTRITION PROFILE

	CALORIES	PROTEIN	FAT	CARBOHYDRATE
9 c. flour	4095	108 gm.	9 gm.	792 gm.
1½ tbsp. yeast	40	6 gm.		6 gm.
¼ c. sugar	192.5			25 gm.
3 c. potato water	?	?		?
	4327.5			

20 loaves, 216.4 calories each. If you make smaller loaves, you can get 28 loaves, 188.4 calories each; 40 loaves, 108 calories each.

PUMPERNICKEL BREAD

This is one of those recipes that should make you jump to your feet, shriek and leap onto the housetop from which, presumably, you might want to shout out the good news. It is chock full of *everything anyone* ever asked for from a loaf of bread!

1½ c. rye flour
2 tsp. salt
2 packages (2 tbsp.) yeast
¼ c. warm water
1½ c. vegetable stock or potato
    water
¼ c. molasses
2 tbsp. oil

1 c. whole-wheat flour
⅓ c. soy grits
2 tbsp. wheat germ
2 tbsp. brewer's yeast
⅓ c. nonfat dried milk
1 egg
2⅔ c. all-purpose unbleached
    flour

PREPARATION

1. Measure all ingredients first. Grease one long pan (13 × 4½ × 2½ in.) or 2 shorter pans (7⅜ × 3⅝ × 2¼ in.).
2. Mix together rye flour, salt, instant yeast (if not instant, dissolve in the water first), warm water and stock, molasses and oil. Beat for 3 minutes.

3. Mix in a separate container whole-wheat flour, soy grits, wheat germ, brewer's yeast, nonfat dried milk.

4. Add egg to first mixture and beat well for 1–2 minutes.

5. Then add the second (dry) mixture to the first and beat very well.

6. Then add 2–3 c. unbleached flour, ½ c. at a time, and mix well after each addition.

7. Turn dough out onto a floured board and knead for 8–10 minutes. Shape into 1 long or 2 small loaves; place in greased pans, cover and let rise in a warm oven (preheated to 140° F. and turned off) until double in size (1–2 hours).

8. Brush top of dough with egg white. Bake in preheated oven at 400° F. for 10 minutes and then reset oven to 350° F. and bake for 30 minutes longer (for large loaf) or 10–20 minutes (for small loaves), until a golden brown on top and lightly brown on the sides. Loaves should leave the sides of the pans easily when turned upside down. Cool on cake racks. This is a solid loaf of bread with a delicious taste and is very filling. Slice thinly and make open-face sandwiches. Yields 40 slices.

NUTRITION PROFILE

	CALO-RIES	PRO-TEIN	FAT	CARBO-HYDRATE
2 packages yeast	40	6 gm.		6 gm.
2 tbsp. brewers yeast	50	6 gm.		6 gm.
¼ c. molasses	200			52 gm.
2 tbsp. oil	250		28 gm.	
1½ c. rye flour	537	16.9 gm.	2.6 gm.	112 gm.
⅓ c. dry milk	23	8 gm.		12 gm.
1 egg	80	6 gm.	6 gm.	
2 tbsp. wheat germ	55	4.5 gm.	1.5 gm.	6.5 gm.
⅓ c. soy grits	43	2.6 gm.	1.9 gm.	3.6 gm.
1 c. whole-wheat flour	400	16 gm.	2 gm.	85 gm.
2⅔ c. un-bleached flour	910	26 gm.	2 gm.	190 gm.
	2588			

40 slices, 64.7 calories/slice. 20 slices, 129.4 calories/slice. 14 slices, each is 184.9 calories/slice. This loaf weighs 889.2 gm. (almost 2 lbs.).

SOURDOUGH, HOMEMADE

I'm not a sourdough fan but I know many who are so here is the basic starter recipe plus an unusual breakfast treat!

SOURDOUGH STARTER

Place 1 c. (8 fl. oz.) whole milk in a glass jar with a loose lid. Allow to stand at room temperature for 24 hours. Then stir in 1 to 1½ c. flour and cover loosely for 2–5 days at room temperature (80° F. is excellent for 2 days, or winter "work" at 60° F. could take 5 days).

HOW TO USE YOUR STARTER

Reserve ¼ c. to use as a base for the next batch. To the remainder, add water at the rate of ½ c. water to 1 c. flour-and-milk mixture (an extra ¼ c. may be needed if the mixture is too firm). Let it bubble another 6–8 hours.

Refrigerate starter between uses. It will keep 2–3 weeks undisturbed but is better if used and refreshed more frequently. This starter can also be frozen for 4–6 months.

SOURDOUGH BREAKFAST PANCAKES

Use 2 c. Sourdough Starter (above) and add to it 1 egg white (whipped lightly), 1 tbsp. safflower oil, 1 tsp. sugar, 2 tbsp. whole milk. Let stand until ready for use.

Add 1 tsp. baking soda to the mix, stir *gently*.

Pour into a Teflon-coated pan lightly greased with oil. Scatter "bacon bits" onto the top with chopped parsley and pepper. Turn, cook second side and serve "bits" side up topped with an egg. Can be made ahead and reheated in the oven before serving. Makes 16–20 pancakes 3–4 in. in diameter.

LEMON YOGURT BREAD

If you make this recipe you might well argue that it seems more like a cake than a bread. You are quite right! If you want an apology—you have it! If you want a "bread" you don't feel you have to smother with butter and jam, then you also have it!

2 tsp. lemon peel, grated
⅓ c. (3 oz.) sugar
¼ c. (4 tbsp.) butter
2 eggs
1 tsp. baking soda

2 c. unbleached flour
1 tsp. baking powder
¼ tsp. salt
1 c. yogurt
1 tsp. vanilla

PREPARATION

1. Finely grate the peel from 1 lemon and measure out 2 tsp.
2. Measure all ingredients. Grease an 8 × 4 × 2 in. loaf pan. Preheat oven to 350° F.
3. Cream butter and sugar well. Sift together flour, salt, baking powder, baking soda. Add eggs one at a time to the butter-sugar mixture and blend well after each addition.
4. Add peel and vanilla flavoring. Alternate adding dry ingredients with the yogurt. Mix until just moistened.
5. Pour into a greased loaf pan and bake for 50 minutes. Cool 10 minutes and turn out onto a wire cake rack to cool completely before cutting, otherwise it will crumble badly. Makes 1 loaf of 20 slices.

NUTRITION AND COST PROFILE

	CALORIES	PROTEIN	FAT	CARBOHYDRATE
⅓ c. sugar	257			66 gm.
¼ c. butter	405	0.5 gm.	45 gm.	0.5 gm.
2 eggs	160	12 gm.	12 gm.	
2 c. flour	840	24 gm.		176 gm.
1 c. yogurt	125	8 gm.	4 gm.	13 gm.

The number of calories per slice is 89.4. The loaf costs about 60¢ to make (3¢ per slice).

31

Poultry

BREAD CASES FOR CASSEROLES

In *The New Seasoning*, I commented upon the difference between a *vol au vent* (puffed pastry case) and a bread case or *croûte* for presenting a small casserole in which little but the actual meat, fish or poultry is used and vegetables are served separately. The case gives the small portion of meat a feeling of bulk and value.

I have used a reformed recipe from the "Galloping Gourmet" days that I named after my wife, Treena—please try it.

BREAD PASTRY CASE
WITH CHICKEN TREENESTAR

1 3–3½ lb. chicken	½ lb. asparagus tips
1 onion	½ c. skim (1%) milk
1 medium whole carrot	2 tbsp. arrowroot
1 bayleaf	1 4½-oz. can of shrimp
3 parsley stalks	1½ tsp. freshly ground salt
3-in. piece of celery	¼ tsp. freshly ground pepper
1 qt. water	1 1-lb. loaf unsliced Italian bread
1 large carrot, thinly sliced	

PREPARATION

1. Place chicken, onion, whole carrot, bayleaf, parsley stalks, and celery in a large dutch oven.

2. Cover with 1 qt. water and simmer gently for 1 hour with the lid on.

3. At the end of 1 hour, remove chicken, separate pieces on a platter to cool quickly and strain the stock. Allow to cool and skim off the surface fat.

4. Cut meat into fork-sized portions, removing skin, bones and cartilage.

5. Measure 1 c. of the chicken stock into a medium-sized saucepan, add sliced carrot, cook 5 minutes, add asparagus, and cook to crisp-tender stage (3–4 minutes).

6. Add milk, mix arrowroot with 2 tbsp. (from the ½ c.) milk and stir in. Bring to a gentle boil, stirring all the time.

7. Add shrimp and chicken and reheat just to the boiling stage.

8. Turn immediately into the toasted and buttered bread case and heat at 250° F. for 10 minutes.

9. *Bread case*: Using standard loaf, slice off the top, leaving a hinge to raise and lower the lid. Raise and support the lid, so it doesn't break off, then scoop out the interior, leaving about ½ in. soft white bread next to the crust. Lightly butter the interior of the loaf, using butter at room temperature. Toast loaf, lid open, for 4 minutes at 350° F. Then fill loaf with chicken mixture and heat, lid closed, for 10 minutes at 250° F. (chicken should be very hot, just prior to filling the loaf). Serve immediately.

NUTRITION PROFILE

	CALORIES	PROTEIN	FAT	CARBOHYDRATE
16 oz. Italian bread	276	26 gm.	13 gm.	170 gm.
1 onion	40	2 gm.		10 gm.
3 lb. chicken	1830	106 gm.	16 gm.	
4½ oz. shrimp	150	35 gm.	2 gm.	2 gm.
1 carrot	20	1 gm.		5 gm.
1 c. stock	30	5 gm.		3 gm.
½ c. 1% milk	45	4.5 gm.		6 gm.
2 tbsp. arrowroot	58			?
½ lb. asparagus	38	3.8 gm.		7.6 gm.
2 tbsp. butter	200		24 gm.	
	2687			

If this serves 6, each serving is 448 calories. If this serves 4, each serving is 672 calories.

Bread case alone: six servings, 46 calories/serving; four servings, 69 calories/serving.

MILD CHICKEN CURRY

I haven't got an asbestos tongue, but I do enjoy a good curry.

1 3½-lb. chicken cut into
  8 pieces
1 medium onion
¼ c. sesame/safflower oil
3 tsp. curry powder
½ tsp. ground chili
3 cloves mashed garlic

6 oz. chicken stock
6 oz. plain yogurt
Freshly ground salt to taste
¼ tsp. ground ginger
Pinch of ground cloves
¼ tsp. black pepper
Pinch ground cumin

PREPARATION

1. Finely slice onion, measure other ingredients.
2. Brown onion in oil in a skillet, then remove to a small dish. Put curry powder, chili, garlic and stock in the oil in the pan. Stir to mix.
3. Add chicken and boil for 20 minutes with lid on.
4. Mix onion and yogurt in the blender, add salt, ginger, cloves, pepper, and cumin and add to the chicken. Stir to mix well.
5. Simmer with lid off for another 15–20 minutes. The chicken is in a lovely sauce and ready to serve. Serves 4.

NUTRITION PROFILE

	CALO-RIES	PRO-TEIN	FAT	CARBO-HYDRATE
1 chicken	690	129 gm.	18 gm.	
¼ c. oil	500		56 gm.	
1 onion	40	2 gm.		10 gm.
6 oz. stock	20	3 gm.		2 gm.
6 oz. plain yogurt	83	5 gm.	3 gm.	9 gm.

Serves 4 at 333 calories per serving.

GINGER-FLAVORED CHICKEN

This recipe sets out to prove only one thing. Ginger is an excellent yet seldom-used spice for chicken, especially when it is roasted.

3½-lb. roasting chicken and
    giblets
2 tbsp. sesame/safflower oil
2 c. water

Freshly ground salt
1 tsp. freshly grated ginger
2 tsp. arrowroot
1 tsp. soy sauce

PREPARATION

1. Chop giblets and brown well in 1 tbsp. hot oil. Cover with 2 c. water, allow to simmer until giblet stock is reduced to 1 c.

2. Season the inside of the chicken with salt and ½ tsp. grated ginger.

3. Tie up chicken. Mix ½ tsp. ginger with 1 tbsp. oil and ½ tsp. salt and brush this mixture over the chicken on both sides.

4. Place giblet stock in roasting pan and place chicken on its side in the stock. Roast for 25 minutes at 375° F.; turn to other side for another 25 minutes, and finally, turn breast up for 10–15 minutes.

5. Skim fat off stock and thicken with a little arrowroot and 1 tsp. soy sauce. Serves 4.

NUTRITION PROFILE

	CALO-RIES	PRO-TEIN	FAT	CARBO-HYDRATE
3½ lbs. chicken	1936	218 gm.	112 gm.	96 gm.
2 tbsp. oil	250		28 gm.	
	2186			

Serves 4 at 546.5 calories/serving or 6 at 364 calories/serving.

HOW TO TRUSS A CHICKEN

If you roast a chicken without trussing it, more of the surface area is exposed, and this leads to evaporation of the juices and to a dry bird. There are also aesthetic advantages in a neatly trussed bird. Well trussed, the bird should be a delectable brown package, compact, plump and yummy; an untrussed bird seems to be awkward, with the legs sticking out at odd angles and the wings about to flap.

There are many ways of trussing a chicken before it is roasted or broiled, but the way I like best uses only a single piece of string and no needles or skewers to pierce the skin. When the skin is pierced it allows the juices to run out, resulting in a much drier bird. With my single-string and single-knot method the truss can easily be removed from the ready-to-serve bird.

Start with butcher's twine. A roll should last about a year, and you will probably need about a yard to truss an average-sized roasting chicken.

1. Find the middle of the string. Place the middle on top of the lower body of the bird with the ends of the string over the drumsticks.

2. Take the right leg, bring it close to the bird's body and wind the string around the bottom drumstick several times. Do the same with the left drumstick and left side of the string.

3. The legs should be secured close to the body, with one thickness of string or twine holding them together at the lower body.

4. Turn the bird over, so that the back is up. Cross the ends of the twine or string over the center back of the bird and loop together. Pull taut.

5. Now bring the strings up to the center of the neck, and the right string goes around the wing, flattening it against the upper back; the left string goes around the left wing, flattening it against the upper left back.

6. Wrapping the twine around the wings, bring the string ends together to tie in a knot to secure the flap of the skin from the neck over the back part of the bird, between the wings.

Note: You can usually get the right kind of twine or string from your local meat market.

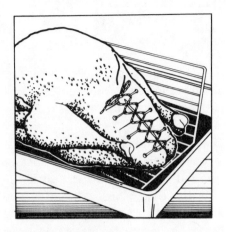

PIN LACE-UP FOR POULTRY

A chicken, when stuffed, has a far juicier texture than a "hollow bird." But how can we fill it and secure the dressing, preventing it from oozing everywhere?

I adopted the "ski-boot" technique of sliding pins through the flesh on either side of the opening and then using one piece of string interlaced tightly (see illustration).

The neck end is securely tied by string.

The best part of this is the ease of removing the string before serving. You extract the pins and lift the string right off.

CHICKEN POLESE

In its original form, this dish came from a small Italian restaurant called Beppie's in Sydney, Australia. The technique it so clearly illustrates is the use of mozzarella cheese in lieu of sauce. Step 7 below shows how the "sauce" is made in only 3 minutes. It saves time and reduces the calorie and fat level compared with Béchamel (rich white sauce).

2 chicken breasts	½ oz. (4 slices) anchovy fillets
1 clove garlic	1 tbsp. sesame / safflower oil
2 tomatoes	2 tsp. Worcestershire sauce
2 oz. green pepper	1 tsp. capers
2 oz. low-fat Mozzarella cheese	Parsley

PREPARATION

1. Remove skin and bones from chicken breasts.

2. Peel and mash garlic; seed, skin and chop tomatoes; cut pepper into thin strips; cut cheese into 2 thin slices; soak anchovies in a little milk, drain and cut lengthwise.

3. Heat oil in a skillet, add chicken and brown on both sides.

4. Add garlic, onion, tomatoes and pepper. Season to taste.

5. Cover skillet and simmer on lowest heat for 30 minutes.

6. At the end of this time, place a slice of cheese and 2 strips of anchovy on top of each chicken breast.

7. Stir Worcestershire sauce in, cover and simmer until cheese melts (3–5 minutes). Place on a heated dish and keep warm.

8. Reduce vegetable pulp and juices until thick (about 5 minutes on medium-high heat). Pour over or around chicken. Sprinkle with capers and parsley and serve.

NUTRITION AND COST PROFILE

	CALO-RIES	PRO-TEIN	FAT	CARBO-HYDRATE
2 chicken breasts	115	20 gm.	3 gm.	
2 tomatoes	40	2 gm.		9 gm.
1 oz. onion	13	0.6 gm.		3 gm.
2 oz. green pepper	7.5	0.5 gm.		2 gm.
¼ oz. anchovy	12.6	1.4 gm.	0.7 gm.	
1 tbsp. oil	125		14 gm.	
2 oz. cheese (low-fat mozzarella)	95	5 gm.	7 gm.	1 gm
	408.1			

Number of calories per serving is 204. Boneless chicken breasts cost $2.39/lb. Price was $2.98 for 4 halves or 75¢ per serving. Breast quarters cost 49¢/lb. Chicken breast, bone in, costs 89¢/lb.

POTATO AND APPLE STUFFING

Many kinds of packaged stuffing mixes are now available in our supermarkets. All of these started out essentially as methods of using excess bread but have grown into industries in themselves. We wanted to see if the potato could be developed into a stuffing and serve the double purpose of a seasoned dressing (which is moisture retaining for the bird) and a starch accompaniment. We based the quantity upon a 3½-lb. roast chicken, which should serve four portions. The stuffing makes 3 c., which is adequate for this roast.

¾ lb. (1½ cups) cooked
   mashed potatoes (2 Idahos =
   1 lb. raw)
1 raw apple, finely diced and
   mixed with 1 tbsp.
   lemon juice

¼ tsp. sage
¼ tsp. thyme
½ tsp. parsley
½ tsp. salt
½ tsp. white pepper

PREPARATION

Boil potatoes. Pour off water and return to a low heat, covering with a towel, and steam dry for 10 minutes. Mash potatoes. Finely chop the apple and mix with the lemon juice. Mix all ingredients together and stuff a 3–4-lb. whole chicken. (See page 209 for pin method of closing.) Rub a little safflower oil over the chicken; salt and pepper to taste. Bake at 350° F. for 1½ hours.

NUTRITION AND COST PROFILE

	CALO-RIES	PRO-TEIN	CARBO-HYDRATE	CAL-CIUM	VITA-MIN A	VITA-MIN C
1 lb. potatoes	279	7.7 gm.	62.8 gm.	26 mg.		73 mg.
1 raw apple	70		18 gm.	8 mg.	5 i.u.	8 mg.
	349					

88 calories per serving. (Bought stuffing mix = 180 calories per serving + 9 gm. fat [butter or margarine] per serving; cost 55¢ per box.)

CHICKEN LIVERS IN "NEW WINE"

These small livers provide an excellent meal that cannot take more than 10 minutes to prepare! The secret is to keep the tender livers only *just* cooked. I would prefer to purchase grain-fed "yard" chicken livers so that I might avoid the chemical seasoning that the battery-bird liver receives. Ask a *good* health food store about purchasing these.

6 oz. sliced onion
Juice of 1 lemon
4 oz. fresh mushrooms
2 tbsp. chopped parsley
4 slices whole-wheat
*   bread, toasted*
16 oz. chicken livers

1 tbsp. butter plus 2 tbsp.
*   sesame/safflower oil*
Freshly ground salt and
*   white pepper*
4 fl. oz. red grape juice
1 tsp. cold, concentrated tea
2 tsp. rice vinegar

FIRST PREPARE

Slice the onion finely, juice the lemon and reserve. Slice mushrooms after washing and drying them. Chop parsley. Toast bread and lightly butter it (optional). Pour lemon juice on mushrooms.

NOW COOK

1. Fry onions and liver in butter and oil for 5 minutes only, no longer.

2. Add mushrooms, lemon juice, salt and pepper. Stir in grape juice and boil rapidly for 1–2 minutes.

3. Add tea and rice vinegar, stirring to keep boiling.

4. Remove from heat, spoon over toast, sprinkle with parsley and serve immediately.

NUTRITION AND COST PROFILE

	CALORIES	PROTEIN	FAT	CARBOHYDRATE
16 oz. chicken livers	693	90.6 gm.	17 gm.	13.3 gm.
4 oz. mushrooms	20	2 gm.		3 gm.
6 oz. onion	62	3 gm.		15.5 gm.
1 lemon	20	1 gm.		6 gm.
4 slices whole-wheat bread	260	12 gm.	4 gm.	56 gm.
1 tbsp. butter	100		12 gm.	
2 tbsp. oil	250		28 gm.	
4 oz. grape juice	82.5			21 gm.

One serving is 372 calories. Chicken livers cost 99¢ per lb., so 4 oz. cost 24.75¢. Mushrooms cost 65¢ per lb., so 4 oz. cost 16.25¢ (1 oz. = 4¢).

Meats

CHILDREN'S MEAT LOAF

Young children are just as entitled to some consideration as adults. Here's a small meat-loaf recipe for them; I would encourage you to let the older daughter or son prepare it for the youngster—it's great fun and fulfills a frequent desire to do something loving and practical for the newest member of the family.

½ lb. calf or pork liver
⅓–1½ c. cooked carrots or
  string beans (optional)
1 tsp. onion (optional)
½ lb. lean ground beef (shin)

⅓ c. tomato puree
⅓ c. milk
1 egg yolk
⅓ c. rolled oats
¼–½ tsp. salt

FIRST PREPARE

Put raw liver, vegetables and onion in the blender and blend on the lowest speed. Add ground beef, tomato puree, milk and egg and blend on a low speed. Turn out into a bowl. Add oats and salt and stir to mix.

NOW COOK

1. Lightly grease an oven-proof dish that holds 1½ pints. Bake at 325° F. for 25–30 minutes, or put into ice cube trays, freeze and

turn out into a freezer baggie. Seal and store in the freezer until needed.

2. Remove one or more meat-loaf cubes and bake in aluminum foil in a 325° F. oven for 15 to 20 minutes. Be sure it is completely cooked. Do not under- or over-cook. Cubes can be mixed with milk or vegetable or meat stock to thin.

Makes 2 cups of uncooked mixture. Each ice cube divider tray holds 2 tbsp. of food. 2 cups of mixture fills 16 divisions.

NUTRITION AND COST PROFILE

	CALO-RIES	PRO-TEIN	FAT	CARBO-HYDRATE
½ lb. pork liver	262	41.2 gm.	7.4 gm.	5.2 gm.
½ lb. beef shin	358	41.4 gm.	20 gm.	
⅓ c. oats	40	2 gm.	1 gm.	8 gm.
⅓ c. tomato puree	97	2 gm.		23 gm.
⅓ c. milk	53	3 gm.	3 gm.	4 gm.
⅓ c. carrots	15			3 gm.
1 egg yolk	60	3 gm.	5 gm.	

Makes 16 2-tbsp. servings at 55.3 calories per serving and costs 6¢/serving (pork liver costs $.49/lb., beef shin costs $1.39/lb.).

BARLEY MEAT LOAF

We have attempted to produce an attractive meat loaf that uses less meat, has higher nutritional value at a lower cost and isn't difficult to make. We think we've done it after 10 different tests using a wide range of ingredients. We used barley to replace part of the meat and a combination of ground beef shin and heel of round that provides meat that is both lean and tasty. The completing sauce is most unusual yet guaranteed to please even conservative tastes.

¼ c. pearl barley
1¼ c. beef stock
1 tbsp. soy sauce
8 oz. ground beef shin
16 oz. ground heel of round
2 oz. diced onion
1 clove garlic, crushed

1 tsp. chopped parsley
¼ tsp. ground pepper
¼ tsp. ground oregano
¼ tsp. ground thyme
2 tbsp. catsup
1 bayleaf
Tomato Sauce (see below)

PREPARATION

1. Simmer barley in beef stock and soy sauce for 1 hour or until tender, and all excess liquid has been absorbed.

2. Measure the rest of the ingredients and mix them together (except the bayleaf and barley). This blends best by hand. Add the barley and stir to blend well.

3. Press mixture into a 4-c. oven-proof container. Place bayleaf on top. Bake at 375° F. for one hour.

4. Drain off into a small saucepan the moisture which forms. Make the Tomato Sauce (below).

5. Turn out Barley Meat Loaf onto a plate, cover with the Tomato Sauce and serve. Makes 4–6 generous servings.

TOMATO SAUCE

¼ c. juice from meat loaf
¼ c. tomato juice
1 tsp. lemon juice

1 tsp. soy sauce
1 tsp. arrowroot
1 tsp. fresh parsley

Place meat juice in a small saucepan and add tomato juice, lemon juice and soy sauce. Heat to almost boiling. Dissolve arrowroot in a little water and stir into the hot mixture. Stir constantly, remove from the heat and add parsley. Pour over turned-out Barley Meat Loaf.

NUTRITION AND COST PROFILE

	CALO-RIES	PRO-TEIN	FAT	CARBO-HYDRATE
24 oz. beef	1320	200 gm.	56 gm.	
¼ c. barley	175	4 gm.	0.5 gm.	39.5 gm.
1¼ c. beef stock	10	4 gm.		2 gm.
2 oz. onion	20	1 gm.		5 gm.
2 tbsp. catsup	30			8 gm.
¼ c. tomato juice	23	11 gm.		2.5 gm.

Serves 4 at 395 calories per serving for 62¢. Serves 6 at 263 calories per serving for 42¢. (Beef shin costs $1.39/lb. Beef heel of round costs between $1.69 and $1.79/lb. 1½ lb. mixed costs $2.49.)

COLD OX TONGUE

One of the really excellent low-cost cuts you can buy is fresh ox tongue. Low in fat yet high in succulence, it is unique for its texture. It is recommended as a good food for babies for ease of digestibility.

A good price per pound is between 90¢ and $1.00. Our test tongue weighed in at 3 lbs. 2 oz. With trim and cooking loss you lose 1 lb. 7 oz., giving 1 lb. 11 oz. at a cost of $1.84 per lb. cooked weight.

The tongue is first soaked in cold water for 1 hour and then rinsed well. Surplus fat and discolored areas are cut away. Then place tongue in a dutch oven to boil with 1 onion, cut in quarters, 1 tsp. salt, 2 bayleaves, 6 peppercorns, 6 cloves of garlic, not crushed, for 4 hours; or pressure cook for 40 minutes and let pressure fall gradually (keep the natural juices for later addition to the finishing sauce).

Skin the tongue and finish off by braising in a 300° F. oven for 1 hour (see next recipe).

BRAISED OX TONGUE

6 oz. mixed vegetables (celery,
   carrots, onions)
1 clove garlic
1 tbsp. oil
1 tbsp. tomato paste
1 tbsp. ham hock stock

1 bayleaf
1 boiled tongue (see page 217)
Tongue cooking liquid
Arrowroot
Parsley

PREPARATION

Blend or chop vegetables and garlic until fine. Fry these fine vegetables in oil and add tomato paste. Cook until the mixture caramelizes. Add the ham hock stock and the bayleaf, stir. Add tongue, cover and braise for 1 hour.

Test tongue by prodding it with a drinking straw—it should be that tender! Strain the sauce, bring to a boil, add the first cooking liquid from the boiled tongue to make 2 c. and thicken with arrowroot (1 tbsp. arrowroot to 2 tbsp. cold water).

Slice the tongue finely and place it in layers on a shallow dish. Coat with the sauce, dust with parsley and serve.

STEAK AU POIVRE

In an effort to reduce the incidence of huge steaks (12 oz. or more per head!) we suggest one large steak, highly seasoned, that can be carved four ways at the table.

24 oz. sirloin or porterhouse
   steak
1 clove garlic, crushed

2 tbsp. whole black peppercorns
1 tbsp. safflower or corn oil
Salt to taste

PREPARATION

1. Wrap garlic in small piece of aluminum foil. Crush garlic with flat edge of French chef's knife. Place peppercorns in an envelope and crush roughly.

2. Rub crushed garlic on both sides of the steak and then remove and discard garlic. Pour pepper out onto a plate and press both sides of the steak into the peppercorns.

3. Pour oil into a frying pan and heat. Lightly salt the steak and fry to desired degree of doneness.

NUTRITION PROFILE

	CALORIES	PROTEIN	FAT
24 oz. sirloin	2640	160 gm.	216 gm.

Serves 4 at 660 calories per serving, 40 gm. protein and 54 gm. saturated fat.

GOOD VERSUS CHOICE PRIME RIBS

Like everyone, we are concerned about ever-increasing beef prices. We are aware that the Choice grade of super-fattened, super-tender aged meat is—or should be—a thing of the past. The leaner, younger grass-fed animal is better in all ways but tenderness, so this helps you to chew more—which is great!

We hope, as we write these details, that you will be able to locate Good grade beef from younger animals, in preference to Choice grade. Our tests indicate substantial savings all the way around.

First we purchased 2 2-rib prime rib roasts weighing 4 lbs. (Choice grade = $2.19 per 1 lb., Good grade = $1.19 per 1 lb.). The difference was found in smaller bones and less fat for the Good grade. We roasted both cuts in the same oven to the same internal temperature of 140° F. This is what we discovered:

	WEIGHT IN	DRIP-PING LOSS	BONES	FAT	MEAT WEIGHT	SLICES	COST PER OZ.
Choice	4 lb. 2 oz.	½ c.	10.5 oz.	16 oz.	1 lb. 15 oz.	11	28.2¢
Good	4 lb. 2 oz.	¼ c.	10 oz.	14 oz.	2 lb. 1 oz.	13	14.4¢

Therefore, you actually save 85¢ a serving! It's better for you, having less fat, and our tests showed no appreciable flavor loss.

COOKING A STANDING RIB ROAST

Some cuts of beef have become real Public Enemies in our lives. The standing rib of beef is a perfect example. Yet I believe it warrants a closer look.

The cut is large and it looks big. It weighs about 4 lbs. when cut to include 2 ribs (the minimum size to purchase). Choice grade at time of writing was $2.19 lb. Thus 4 lb. cost $8.76. We get 1 lb. 5 oz. trimmed meat, or 11 good slices serving 5 people with excellent portions of 6 oz. each at a cost of $1.75 per portion with all fat trimmed off (14 oz. fat) and the bones (10½ oz.) to be used for stock.

Certainly it's a treat, and because of this it is essential to treat it with great care. Roast not a degree over 325° F. I roasted an identical cut at 385° F. and look at the difference:

CUT	WEIGHT	TEMPERA-TURE	COOKING TIME	INTERNAL TEMPERA-TURE
A) 2 ribs	4 lb. 2 oz.	325°F.	120 minutes	140°F.
B) 2 ribs	4 lb. 2 oz.	385°F.	110 minutes	140°F.

	PAN GREASE	WEIGHT OUT	BONE WEIGHT	FAT TRIM*
A)	½ c.	3 lb. 13 oz.	10½ oz.	14 oz.
B)	⅔ c.	3 lb. 3 oz.	11½ oz.	16 oz.

	PURE MEAT	NO. SLICES	COST PER OZ.
A)	1 lb. 15 oz.	11	28.2¢
B)	1 lb. 7 oz.	8	38 ¢

* Contains some meat layers that were not removed in either case.

Rub a little salt and freshly ground black pepper into the meat, cut a little pocket between the ribs and push a garlic clove up into the incision. Then rest the roast (standing fat uppermost) on the bones in an ovenproof roasting pan. Place roast in an oven set at 325° F. and roast to an internal temperature of 140° F., tested with a good meat thermometer. Don't add any fat; it has plenty of its own. Turn the oven off. Let the cut stand in oven with door open for 20 minutes before carving. This way you will get outside end slices well done, inside medium, and middle slices rare.

CARVING A RIB ROAST OF BEEF

Carving a small roast prime rib of beef has more to it than meets the eye.

There are four things to look out for: setting, fat and bone removal, heat and slice size.

Setting. Each roast should be internally measured to 140° F. and then allowed to set in an open oven turned *off* for 20 minutes before carving. It will be easier to handle this way.

Fat. We get between 14 and 16 oz. of solid fat off a 4-lb. rib roast. This must come off. It represents close to 3000 calories or 200 calories per oz. of saturated fat. The bones are also removed for ease of carving, and they make excellent stock.

Heat. Slices should be carved onto a heated dish.

Slice size. We highly recommend thin slices for better flavor. Smaller pieces also look better on the plate and are easier to cut, chew and swallow.

STEAK: SALT BEFORE OR AFTER?

More concern has been expressed on when to season than on almost any other facet of meat cookery.

We conducted experiments to test the validity of the claims that juices are drawn out by the salt, that the finished color is impaired and that the meat is toughened—serious allegations, to be sure. We cut identical slices of beef and seasoned each piece with salt only: no. 1 salted 5 minutes before cooking, no. 2 salted in the pan. The juice loss was not significant, the color was unchanged and the taste was better with the advanced seasoning. "Toughness" appeared also to be unchanged.

As a result, we recommend that steak be properly seasoned before cooking by massaging a *small* quantity of salt into the flesh.

QUICK SAUERBRATEN

Sauerbraten is a marinated block of beef that is then braised and served fork tender and juicy. The cost in calories per serving is a shade over 550, which makes it the villain of this volume, but on the other hand it is a good rib-sticking repast for the hungry man—especially after a day in the snow.

2½ lb. beef chuck
½ c. rice vinegar
2 tbsp. lemon juice
½ c. water
½ c. red grape juice
1 tbsp. safflower oil
1 clove garlic, crushed
2 tbsp. tomato paste

Salt and pepper to taste
1 tsp. fresh or ¼ tsp. ground
  ginger
2 bayleaves
2 onions cut into quarters
1 tbsp. cold tea
2 tbsp. arrowroot in 2 tbsp.
  water

FIRST PREPARE

Marinate meat in vinegar, lemon juice, water and grape juice for 2 hours. Do not use an aluminum pot for either marinating or cooking the meat. Measure or otherwise prepare other ingredients before cooking.

NOW COOK

1. Dry off meat, brown in a dutch oven in the oil, then add the garlic, tomato paste, and further brown until paste is caramelized.
2. Add salt, pepper, ginger, bayleaves, onions, cold tea, and the marinade to the pot.
3. Cover and cook gently for 1½–2 hours.
4. Remove the meat from the pot and place on a warmed platter. Slice the meat and keep warm while thickening the sauce.
5. Strain the marinade stock and return to the heat. When it boils, remove from the heat, stir in the arrowroot cream and return to the heat. Stir constantly until it boils again and thickens. Remove from the heat immediately. Spoon a little over the meat and place the rest in a gravy bowl to serve at the side. Serves 4.

NUTRITION PROFILE

	CALORIES	PROTEIN	FAT	CARBOHYDRATE
2½ lbs. lean beef	1862	292.6 gm.	66.5 gm.	
½ c. vinegar				8 gm.
2 tbsp. lemon juice	7.5			2 gm.
½ c. grape juice	82.5	0.5 gm.		21 gm.
1 tbsp. oil	125		14 gm.	
2 onions	80	4 gm.		8 gm.
2 tbsp. tomato paste	58			?
2 tbsp. arrowroot				
	2215			

Using lean beef, the dish has 554 calories per serving.

PORK SHISHKEBAB

Quite apart from the convenience of handling a quantity of cubed meat, the skewer has the added advantage of allowing a maximum area to be coated in a glaze resulting from radiant heat playing directly upon a marinated surface. Try this simple idea that uses only ordinary kitchen equipment.

Marinade
2 tbsp. soy sauce
1 tbsp. rice vinegar
¼ tsp. fresh gingerroot
1 clove garlic, crushed
2–3 tbsp. water
Garnish
4 cups cooked long-grain rice

1½ lbs. loin cut pork, bone out
* (or pork butt)*
4 skewers
Aluminum foil
9 in. round or square cake pan
vegetables (optional)
1 tbsp. oil

PREPARATION

1. Measure and combine marinade ingredients. Use marinade only with pork butt; not needed with loin cut. Cut meat into ½ in. chunks. Soak meat in marinade mixture several hours or overnight. Be sure there is enough marinade to cover the meat.

2. Line the cake pan with foil. Put 5–6 oz. of meat on each skewer. Place pan with skewers laid rim-to-rim on top, under the broiler. The fat will drip down. Turn every 5 minutes (10–15 minutes total cooking time).

3. Cut vegetables to be eaten with meat into 1–1½-inch squares. Pan-fry them in 1 tbsp. oil to the crisp-tender stage.

Serve bowls of hot vegetables to be dipped in different mustard, chili or soy sauces or mixed with the meat, which has been pushed off the skewers onto a bed of rice. This is a very versatile meat, at 620 calories per serving.

COST PROFILE

Foods can be skewered under the broiler, so an extra piece of apparatus is not necessary. Wooden, disposable skewers cost 69¢ for 100 eight-inch bamboo pieces. Metal reusable ones cost $1.00 apiece or more, but the metal helps to cook the meat more quickly. Meat *only* is placed on skewers; small, 1-in. chunks looked and tasted best. We used pork loin ($1.19 per lb.) and pork butt ($1.29) for our comparison. We marinated the pork butt, but not the loin.

33 ————————————————

Desserts

APPLE-LEMON SOUFFLÉ

Desserts are of real value following a meal only if they delight and freshen, not saturate and make heavy. This soufflé is definitely a freshener!

2 envelopes unflavored gelatin
2 c. cold water
4 tsp. grated lemon peel
3 tbsp. sugar
pinch of salt
2 apples, pared, cored and
grated (Granny Smiths
are good)

juice of 1 lemon (¼ c.)
4 egg whites
8 oz. plain yogurt
2 tbsp. wheat germ

Use a regular soufflé dish or a 7 in. or smaller springform pan.

PREPARATION

1. Assemble all ingredients; do not grate apples until the last possible moment. Bring egg whites to room temperature.
2. Sprinkle gelatin over ½ c. cold water in a small saucepan. Stir over low heat to dissolve.
3. Remove saucepan from heat. Stir in grated lemon peel, sugar, salt and remaining 1½ c. cold water.
4. Chill gelatin until syrupy. Then beat gelatin until foamy.

5. Grate apples, cover and toss well with lemon juice. Fold grated apples into gelatin.

6. Beat egg whites until stiff but not dry. Fold egg whites into gelatin mixture and pour into greased, prepared pan. Refrigerate 3 hours or until firm.

7. Just before serving, unmold and frost with 8 oz. plain yogurt. Dust with 2 tbsp. wheat germ. Serve immediately. Serves 8.

NUTRITION PROFILE

	CALO-RIES	PRO-TEIN	FAT	CARBO-HYDRATE
2 envelopes gelatin	50	12 gm.		
3 tbsp. sugar	120			33 gm.
1 lemon	20	1 gm.		6 gm.
4 egg whites	60	16 gm.		
2 apples	140			36 gm.
2 tbsp. wheat germ	55	4.5 gm.	1.5 gm.	6.5 gm.
8 oz. plain yogurt	125	8 gm.	4 gm.	1.3 gm.
	570			

If 8 servings, then 71 calories/serving. If 6 servings, then 95 calories/serving.

INFANT DESSERT

If we are concerned about one another, if we love one another, then how much more should we care for the very young.

Commercial baby foods use extenders, flavor enhancers and preservatives because their aim is a 3-year shelf life. To achieve this they add between 5 and 60 times the amount of salt suited to babies, they add sugar, formerly MSG (now banned), modified starch (indigestible) and nitrates. All this is added only to please the mother, because the infant does not readily taste salt or sweet before the age of 7 months. Hence we present our infant dessert for *you* to make from natural, wholesome ingredients.

BABY'S FRUIT GELATIN DESSERT

1 tbsp. unflavored gelatin
¼ c. cold water
1⅓ c. fresh orange juice
   (3 temple oranges were
   just right)

⅔ c. water
2 oz. ripe banana, sliced

FIRST PREPARE

Squeeze orange juice. Measure other ingredients.

NOW COOK

1. Place cold water in a small saucepan. Add gelatin, stir and heat gently to just dissolve gelatin granules.

2. Place orange juice, ⅔ c. water, banana slices and gelatin mixture in a blender and blend for 15–25 seconds on the lowest speed.

3. Pour into small custard cups and refrigerate until used. Makes 8 servings of about ⅓ c. each. Do not store for longer than 1 week.

NUTRITION PROFILE

This could be fed to a baby from 3 or 4 months old on. As the baby gets older, the ⅔ cup water can be replaced with all orange juice or other types of juices except fresh or frozen pineapple juice. This is much healthier for the child than artificially flavored and colored, oversweetened, premixed gelatin desserts.

	CALO-RIES	PRO-TEIN	FAT	CARBO-HYDRATE
1 pkg. unflavored gelatin	25	6 gm.		
1⅓ c. orange juice	147	3 gm.	1 gm.	35 gm.
2 oz. banana	30			9 gm.
	202			

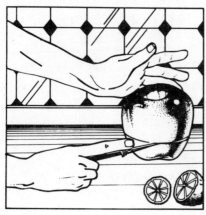

BAKED APPLES

So many of our dishes served as desserts are surrounded by a cloud of carbohydrate or smothered in cream! Here is a good recipe that traces almost all its calories to pure healthy fruit.

4 firm McIntosh apples
Juice of ½ lemon
4 tbsp. oatmeal, dry

Scant ¼ tsp. ground allspice
16 pitted, plumped prunes

PREPARATION

1. Core apples and score the skin all around the equator of the apple, about 1 in. up from the bottom (see illustration).
2. Rub lemon juice inside the cut surface.
3. Set apples in a shallow baking dish.
4. Place prunes in water that has been brought to a boil and simmer for 10 minutes to plump. Remove pits and mash prunes with a fork or spoon. Add allspice and mash; stir in oatmeal. Fill each apple just to the top with this mixture.
5. Bake at 350° F. for 45 minutes. Serve immediately.

NUTRITION PROFILE

	CALO- RIES	PRO- TEIN	CARBO- HYDRATE
4 apples	280		18 gm.
4 tbsp. oatmeal	32		1.4 gm.
16 prunes	280	1 gm.	18 gm.
	592		

One serving has 148 calories.

LOW-CALORIE CHEESECAKE

Cheesecake is one of those desserts I order when I'm in an extreme state of diet rebellion. Because of this we decided to produce a "low-impact cheesecake." We were excited about this project and when we eventually discovered the method that gave us a 198-calorie slice against the regular 456-calorie slice, we rejoiced. I believe that much can be done by adding to this base and I do urge you to experiment with adding raisins or chopped dates. You can also stir in a little blue cheese—you name it—it's a creative possibility!

1¼ c. graham cracker crumbs
¼ c. melted butter
2 tbsp. cold water
2 tbsp. lemon juice
1 envelope unflavored gelatin

½ c. nonfat dried milk,
  liquefied and heated to boiling
1 whole egg
⅓ c. sugar
2 c. low-fat cottage cheese
1 tsp. vanilla flavoring

CRUST

Place graham crackers in blender and whiz until fine. Melt margarine. Blend together and press into a 9-in. pie plate.

FILLING

Place cold water with lemon juice and gelatin into blender, cover and process at low speed to soften gelatin. Remove feeder cap and add boiling milk. When gelatin is dissolved, turn to highest speed. Add remaining ingredients and continue to process until smooth. Pour mixture into graham cracker crust. Refrigerate 2–3 hours before serving.

NUTRITION PROFILE

	CALO-RIES	PRO-TEIN	SATU-RATED FAT	CARBO-HYDRATE	VITA-MIN A	CAL-CIUM
1¼ c. graham crackers	495	9 gm.		94.5 gm.		
4 tbsp. butter	408		48 gm.			
Gelatin	25	6 gm.				
1 egg	80	6 gm.	2 gm.		590 i.u.	27 mg.
½ c. nonfat dried milk	45	4.5 gm.		6 gm.	10 i.u.	148 mg.
⅓ c. sugar	257			66.6 gm.		
2 c. low-fat cottage cheese	276	68 gm.		10 gm.	20 i.u.	360 mg.
	1586					

Serves 8 at 198 calories per slice.

LOW-CALORIE REFORM CUSTARD

A good egg custard can be made much less of a menace by reducing butterfat, egg yolks and sugar, but what would it taste like? You guessed it—not much!

1½ c. nonfat dried milk,
  liquefied
1 tbsp. sugar

3 egg yolks
1 vanilla pod, uncut
2 tsp. arrowroot

PREPARATION

Reconstitute the dried milk at the rate of ⅓ c. plus 2 tbsp. per c. water. Reserve 2 tbsp. liquefied milk to mix with the arrowroot.

To the remaining milk, add the sugar, egg yolks and the vanilla pod (uncut, because otherwise the fine seeds would spill out and spoil the appearance of the custard). Stir well and place in the top of a double boiler. Heat to 190° F. Cook 10 minutes over boiling water. Add the arrowroot mixed with the reserved cold milk and stir into the hot mixture. Continue stirring until the custard thickens.

If served plain, you may need to add a little sugar (1 tbsp. maximum), or try 1 tsp. decaffeinated instant coffee and no extra sugar. Serve ice cold. Makes 2 cups (16 oz.).

NUTRITION PROFILE

	CALO-RIES	PROTEIN	FAT
1½ c. nonfat dried milk	170	18 gm.	trace
3 egg yolks	360	9 gm.	15 gm.
1 tbsp. sugar	40		
2 tsp. arrowroot	10		
	580		

One ½-c. serving is 145 calories.

PAPUFA WHIPPED TOPPING

The word *papufa* means Physiologically Active Polyunsaturated Fatty Acid. This topping is suited to low-cholesterol diets. It replaces artificial toppings and costs next to nothing.

½ c. ice water
½ c. nonfat dried milk (1½ oz.)
3 tbsp. sugar

1 tbsp. safflower oil
½ tsp. vanilla extract

FIRST PREPARE

Place mixing bowl in freezer. Fill a larger bowl ⅓ full with ice cubes and water. Measure out all ingredients. Place ½ c. ice water and milk in chilled bowl and place this bowl in the larger bowl. Mix at high speed with an electric beater until stiff peaks form (7–10 minutes). After peaks form, add the sugar, 1 tbsp. at a time, beating well after each addition. Add the oil slowly and beat well. Finally add the vanilla and beat only enough to mix. Yields 3 c. whipped topping.

NUTRITION PROFILE

	CALORIES	PROTEIN	FAT	CARBOHYDRATE
½ c. nonfat dried milk	122.5	12 gm.		17.5 gm.
3 tbsp. sugar	80			33 gm.
1 tbsp. safflower oil	125		14 gm.	

Commercial toppings contain 175–230 calories per c. with 12–20 gm. fat per c. Ours weighs in at 109 calories per c. and 4.6 gm. fat per c.

FOURTH OF JULY PARFAIT

This is a fun dessert originally developed to celebrate 1976. In addition to being fun and obviously patriotic (it is red, white and blue), it is high in protein, low in fat and costs only 236 calories for a giant feast!

Enjoy and congratulations on being over 200 years old!

4 8-oz. cartons plain yogurt
⅔ c. well-drained strawberries
⅔ c. blueberries
2 tbsp. plus 2 tsp. honey

½ tsp. vanilla extract
2 drops blue food coloring
4 tsp. wheat germ

PREPARATION

1. Mash berries in 2 separate bowls.
2. To the strawberries add 1 tbsp. honey and 1⅓ c. yogurt. Stir to mix. Set aside.
3. To the blueberries add 1 tbsp. honey and 1⅓ c. yogurt. Stir to blend. Set aside.
4. To the final 1⅓ c. yogurt add 2 tsp. honey and ½ tsp. vanilla.
5. Layer the 3 fillings in 4 parfait glasses, starting with the blue-

berry, then the vanilla and finally the strawberry layer. The second and third layers must be poured in very carefully, or they sink into the first layer. We bent a teaspoon upward to form an L at about a 100° angle, and poured the top 2 layers onto the spoon and allowed it to spill over and cover the first and second layers.

6. Garnish with 1 tsp. wheat germ sprinkled over the top of each parfait. Serves 4.

NUTRITION PROFILE

	CALORIES	PROTEIN	FAT	CARBOHYDRATE
4 c. plain yogurt	500	32 gm.	16 gm.	52 gm.
⅔ c. blueberries	57	1 gm.	1 gm.	14 gm.
⅔ c. strawberries	186	1 gm.	1 gm.	47 gm.
8 tsp. honey	173			45 gm.
4 tsp. wheat germ	27	2 gm.	1 gm.	3 gm.
	943			

One serving has 236 calories.

NO-CRUST APPLE PIE

This recipe takes much less time than a pastry-crust pie. The calories are greatly reduced and the taste is wonderful. The only negative is appearance. We find that a good blob of yogurt helps, or you could try Papufa Topping (page 231).

4 cooking apples	1 tbsp. wheat germ
½ c. dry oatmeal	2 tbsp. brown sugar
1 tbsp. coconut	1 tsp. cinnamon
2 tbsp. sliced almonds	2 tbsp. melted butter

PREPARATION

Melt butter. Measure out other ingredients, except apples, into a medium-sized mixing bowl. Pour butter over the mixture and stir to blend. Peel and slice apples in a 9-in. pie plate. Sprinkle coarse mixture over the apples and bake at 375° F. for 25 minutes. Serve warm as is, or with skim milk or a dollop of yogurt or Papufa. Serves 6.

NUTRITION PROFILE

	CALORIES	PROTEIN	FAT	CARBOHYDRATE
4 apples	280			72 gm.
½ c. oats	65	2.5 gm.	1 gm.	11 gm.
1 tbsp. coconut	27		2 gm.	2.6 gm.
2 tbsp. almonds	53	1.6 gm.	4.8 gm.	1.8 gm.
1 tbsp. wheat germ	27	2 gm.	1 gm.	3 gm.
2 tbsp. brown sugar	51			13 gm.
2 tbsp. butter	200		24 gm.	
	703			

One serving is 117 calories.

RICE PUDDING

Milk puddings provide a splendid dessert, filling, satisfying, inexpensive and nutritious. One of the easiest is rice pudding. For this you need short-grain rice, such as Carolina—long grain will not work.

4 oz. (½ c.) dry rice	1 vanilla pod
4 c. 2% milk	2 tbsp. granulated sugar
2 pieces lemon peel (1 x 2 in.)	1 medium egg

Place rice, milk, lemon peel and vanilla in a medium-large saucepan. Raise to the boil and simmer for 20 minutes uncovered on very low heat. Remove lemon peel, add sugar, stir in well and let the mixture cool naturally. Then chill. Beat egg white, stir into egg yolk and fold this mixture into rice. Serve in parfait glasses with a colorful fruit topping. Serves 4.

TAPIOCA PUDDING

Tapioca is made from the roots of the cassava or manioc plant. It is *very* digestible; recommended for babies and elderly persons.

⅓ c. pearl tapioca	1 egg
2¼ c. milk	¼ c. sugar
¼ tsp. salt	¼ tsp. vanilla extract
1 tbsp. arrowroot	cinnamon
2 tbsp. milk	

FIRST PREPARE

Soak the pearl tapioca for 3 hours in ¾ c. water.

NOW COOK

Pour off water from tapioca. Add 2¼ c. milk and salt and place mixture in a 1½-qt. saucepan (nonstick is best). Heat and stir until it boils. Simmer uncovered, stirring frequently, over lowest possible heat for 50 minutes. Mix the arrowroot and 2 tbsp. milk, pour into the hot mixture and bring to a boil, stirring constantly; reduce heat. Beat the egg, sugar and vanilla extract together. Mix about ½ to ¾ c. of the hot tapioca with the egg, then pour mixture back into the saucepan. Stir rapidly to mix. Remove from heat. Serve hot or chilled, in small glasses and dusted with cinnamon.

NUTRITION PROFILE

	CALO-RIES	PRO-TEIN	SATU-RATED FAT	CAL-CIUM	VITA-MIN A
⅓ c. tapioca	178			43.7 mg.	0.2 i.u.
2¼ c. milk	326	20.25 gm.	12.5 gm.	648 mg.	787.5 i.u.
1 tbsp. arrowroot	29				
1 egg	80	6 gm.	2 gm.	27 mg.	590 i.u.
¼ c. sugar	192.5				
	805.5				

This recipe makes 3¼ c. at 124 calories per ½-c. serving, somewhat less than regular tapioca (140 calories).

BREAD AND BUTTER PUDDING

We have tried hard to reform this dessert largely because it is so good. We severely reduced the sugar and strove to make this up with dried fruit as a more satisfactory source of sweetness. Note the serving size if you are concerned about caloric restriction.

2 oz. butter at room
temperature
3 tbsp. sugar
3 slices white bread
3 slices whole-wheat bread
2½ c. skim milk

½ vanilla pod
2 pieces thin lemon peel
2 oz. seedless raisins or currants
2 oz. candied lemon peel
3 eggs
Nutmeg

FIRST PREPARE

Out of the 2 oz. butter, lightly butter the inside of a 2-qt. casserole and dust it with ½ tbsp. of the sugar. Preheat oven to 325° F. Spread the bread lightly with the rest of the butter and cut the slices in half diagonally. Measure the remaining ingredients.

NOW COOK

1. Place milk, vanilla pod, fresh lemon peel and 2 tbsp. sugar in a saucepan and scald.

2. Stir to dissolve sugar.

3. Arrange some of the cut bread on the bottom of the casserole.

4. Sprinkle it with some of the raisins and candied peel.

5. Place another layer of bread over the first layer, alternating brown and white layers.

6. Break eggs into a bowl and whisk.

7. Slowly beat in the scalded milk, having first removed the lemon peel and vanilla pod.

8. Pour this mixture over the bread, dust with ½ tbsp. sugar and nutmeg.

9. Bake in preheated 325° F. oven for 35 minutes. Serve warm, with milk or plain. Serves 6–8.

NUTRITION PROFILE

	CALO-RIES	PRO-TEIN	FAT	CARBO-HYDRATE
3 eggs	240	18 gm.	18 gm.	
2½ c. milk	225	22.5 gm.		30 gm.
3 tbsp. sugar	120			33 gm.
3 slices white bread	210	6 gm.	3 gm.	39 gm.
3 slices w/w bread	195	9 gm.	3 gm.	42 gm.
2 oz. raisins	160			44 gm.
2 oz. candied peel	150			4.5 gm.
2 oz. butter	400		48 gm.	
	1700			

Serves 8 at 213 calories or 6 at 283 calories.

Fruit

APRICOTS AND MACE

Dried fruits plus spice and water only can be delicious. Try the recipe below and add whipped egg white for a low-calorie, sugar-free dessert. The sweet-tasting mace replaces the sugar.

1 c. dried (sulfur-free) apricots　　　*½ tsp. mace, grated*
1 c. water

PREPARATION

1. Measure out apricots and water; grate mace and measure ½ tsp.
2. Place fruit in a glass saucepan with an equal amount of water.
3. Bring fruit to a boil. Sprinkle grated mace on top, cover and simmer gently for 10 minutes. Remove from heat and allow to cool. Most of the moisture should be absorbed. Makes 1½ c.

NUTRITION AND COST PROFILE

	CALO-RIES	PRO-TEIN	FAT	CARBO-HYDRATE	CAL-CIUM	IRON	VITA-MIN A	VITA-MIN C	NIACIN
5 oz. apricots	368	8 gm.	1 gm.	100 gm.	100 mg.	8.2 mg.	16,350 i.u.	19 mg.	4.9 mg.

5 oz. dry equals 1 cup; 9 oz. cooked equals 1 cup.

Cost: $2.39 for 11 oz. or 22¢ per oz. A cheaper variety cost 99¢ for 8 oz. or 12¢ per oz., but were moldy and had stems left on them, and were much smaller.

SWEDISH FRUIT BLOOP SOUP

This is great fun, almost a meal in itself, and greatly enjoyed by young and old alike. It's called *bloop* because of its habit of throwing spoonfuls of puree into the air as it boils in step 2. Hence the double boiler in step 4!

1 c. dried peaches
1 c. dried apricots
½ c. dried apples
½ c. pitted prunes
½ #30 can red tart
  pitted cherries
¼ c. raisins
1 qt. water
1-in. piece cinnamon

½ tsp. lemon peel, freshly
  grated
⅛ tsp. ground mace
Dash each of cardamom, ground
  allspice, ground nutmeg
1¼ c. buttermilk
5 tbsp. yogurt
1 tsp. nutmeg

PREPARATION

1. Measure or otherwise prepare all ingredients.
2. In a large saucepan combine all ingredients except buttermilk, yogurt and 1 tsp. nutmeg. Bring to a boil, reduce heat, cover and simmer gently for 1 hour.
3. Remove cinnamon. Place soup in a blender and purée.
4. Return soup to a double boiler, reheat with the buttermilk.
5. Ladle soup into bowls. Garnish with 1 tbsp. yogurt and a dash of nutmeg and serve hot. Serves 6.

NUTRITION PROFILE

	CALO-RIES	PRO-TEIN	FAT	CARBO-HYDRATE
1 c. dried peaches	420	5 gm.	1 gm.	109 gm.
1 c. dried apricots	390	8 gm.	1 gm.	100 gm.
½ c. dried apples	177	0.7 gm.	1 gm.	46 gm.
½ c. pitted prunes	140	2 gm.		36 gm.
½ c. canned cherries	105	2 gm.		26 gm.
¼ c. raisins	80			22 gm.
1¼ c. buttermilk	112	11 gm.		15 gm.
5 tbsp. yogurt	63	4 gm.	2 gm.	6 gm.
	1487			

Serves 6 at 248 calories per serving, 3.8 mg. iron, 4201 I.U. vitamin A, 11.5 mg. vitamin C, 8 gm. protein.

FRUIT CURRY

We offer this Fruit Curry to those with a taste for the unusual.

2 lbs. mixed fruit (not citrus) cut into 1 in. pieces
1 tbsp. oil
2 oz. onion, finely chopped
2 tsp. mild curry powder
1 tsp. ground ginger or 1 tbsp. freshly grated ginger

1 pt. veal stock
1 tbsp. arrowroot
Salt
3 oz. desiccated coconut liquid
Juice of 1 lemon
½ c. light cream

PREPARATION

1. Use pineapple, peaches, pears, plums, etc. If fruit is in cans, there is no need to cook it. Otherwise poach fruit until semi-cooked. Measure or otherwise prepare other ingredients.

2. Put oil in frying pan and lightly sauté onions, but do not let them get brown or hard (just to transparent stage).

3. Add curry powder and fry 1 minute longer. Add ginger and stir to mix. Add veal stock, bring to a boil and reduce by half the original volume. Thicken with arrowroot dissolved in a little cold water.

4. Add salt to taste, but keep to an absolute minimum. Add fruit and boil for a few minutes.

5. Add the coconut liquid and lemon juice, mix well but *do not boil*, and finally stir in the cream.

6. Serve with plain boiled rice—hot Fruit Curry in the winter and cold Fruit Curry in the summer. Makes 4–6 servings.

NUTRITION PROFILE

	CALO-RIES	PRO-TEIN	FAT	CARBO-HYDRATE
8 oz. pineapple	135	1 gm.		34 gm.
8 oz. peaches	75	1 gm.		20 gm.
8 oz. pears	120	1 gm.	1 gm.	40 gm.
8 oz. plums	100	1 gm.		24 gm.
1 tbsp oil	125		14 gm.	
1 tbsp. arrowroot	28			?
1 pt. veal stock	60	5 gm.		6 gm.
3 oz. coconut liquid	252	3.2 gm.	24.9 gm	5.2 gm.
1 lemon	20	1 gm.		6 gm.
½ c. light cream	252	3.5 gm.	25 gm.	5 gm.
	1167			

Serves 4 generously at 292 calories per serving.

BROILED GRAPEFRUIT

This is our lowest calorie dessert and I highly recommend it to you. The cardamom and grape juice will add enough "new" flavor interest to replace the usual kirsch or other liqueur.

2 pink grapefruit
2 tbsp. white grape juice

1 tsp. rice vinegar
Dash of ground cardamom

PREPARATION

1. Cut grapefruit in half. Loosen and remove cores and cut around each segment to loosen it.

2. Place grapefruit on a heatproof plate and broil 4 in. away from the unit for 5 minutes.

3. While the grapefruit are broiling, heat the grape juice and vinegar to almost boiling. Pour the liquid over the grapefruit; dust very gently with a little cardamom and serve immediately. Serves 4.

NUTRITION PROFILE

	CALO-RIES	PRO-TEIN	FAT	CARBO-HYDRATE
½ grapefruit	50	1 gm.		13 gm.
½ tbsp. grape juice	5			1.3 gm.
	55			

Pink grapefruit has much more vitamin A than white grapefruit (½ white grapefruit = 10 I.U. vitamin A; ½ pink grapefruit = 540 I.U. vitamin A).

A NEW BREAKFAST: HI-FI CEREAL

We are delighted with the high-fiber diets showing up everywhere and have adopted various personal approaches. Treena eats ½ oz. bran flakes with 3 oz. fresh orange juice; George (a friend) adds 1 tbsp. bran flakes to yogurt and apricot juice; and I mix bran with 2 tbsp. frozen black raspberries and 3 oz. milk. But we all like the following recipe.

See also our comments on cereals on page 76.

HI-FI CEREAL

¾ c. 100% bran cereal
6 tbsp. sunflower seeds
¾ c. black raspberries

1 apple, skin included
½ c. prunes, dry or cooked

PREPARATION

1. Measure out all ingredients. Wash and grate apple.
2. Cook prunes, if so desired.
3. Mix all ingredients in a medium-sized mixing bowl.
4. Allow mixture to sit for about 5 minutes to allow bran to soak up the liquid.
5. Serve in ½-c. servings. Makes 2-plus c. Serve plain or with milk, buttermilk or yogurt.

NUTRITION PROFILE

	CALO-RIES	PRO-TEIN	FAT	FIBER
¾ c. (1½ oz.) bran cereal	120	6.3 gm.	1.5 gm.	3 gm.
6 tbsp. sunflower seeds	560	24 gm.	47 gm.	1.95 gm.
¾ c. black raspberries	53			5.7 gm.
1 apple	70			1.5 gm.
½ c. (8) prunes	140	2 gm.		1.2 gm.
	943			13.35 gm.

Without milk, each serving has 236 calories and 3.34 gm. crude fiber. With ½ c. skim milk, one serving has 281 calories (½ c. skim milk = 45 calories and 4.5 gm. protein).

NO-COOK PEACH JAM

Jams and other sweetened preserves hit our bodies with a huge load of sugar at breakfast time—at 55 calories per *level* teaspoon. I set out to reduce the recipe for a No-Cook Peach Jam from 5 c. sugar (770 calories per c. = 3850 calories) to 2 c. sugar, a saving of 2310 calories.

9 *fresh peaches, peeled*
Juice of 1 lemon
2 c. sugar

1 package (1¾ oz.) powdered
pectin in ½ c. water
1 envelope gelatin in
¼ c. warm water

PREPARATION

Peel and pit peaches. Chop in blender at lowest speed (fruit will be lumpy). Add the lemon juice. Stir in the sugar and let stand for 10 minutes. In a saucepan, stir the pectin into ½ c. water. Bring to a boil over medium heat, stir constantly for 1 minute, then add to fruit and stir for 3 minutes.

Dissolve the gelatin in ¼ c. warm water and stir until clear. Add to the fruit and stir well. Pour into jars and place in the refrigerator for 8–12 hours to harden. The jam may be refrigerated up to 3 weeks or frozen for 6 months. Makes approximately 2 c. jam.

CUTTING LEMONS

I am quite tired of poorly cut citrus fruit—it seems like a fearful waste of money to cut thin disks that cannot season. So I will explain how to do a really good job on our expensive friend.

Lemons rise in price but never fall in virtue. With price increase, we need waste decrease. These are some ideas:

1. Purchase a "lemon notcher," a utensil that cuts grooves in a whole lemon. This makes it easier to get a firm squeeze. It utilizes

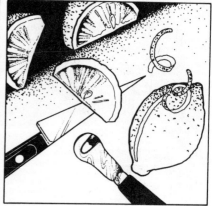

some of the peel for special dishes and seasonings: Just blanch the thin strips by placing them into cold water and bringing them to a boil, then dry them out in an oven set at 200° F. for 20 minutes. Bottle and keep for future use; it's attractive!

2. After notching, cut lemons into quarters and trim the ends flat for a better grip. Also, roll them first to get the juice loosened up. One wedge should produce 1 tsp. without effort (50% increase in juice over nonrolled).

3. Do not use the screw-in juicer. It is a good-looking gadget, but you get only 70% of the juice you can get from a regular lemon squeezer.

MATURING TREE FRUIT AT HOME

We have found that very hard fruit may be brought to edible maturity in 1–2 days by placing the fruit in a plastic bag with a green apple. Not only is maturity hastened, but the flavor is markedly improved.

Peaches, apricots, kiwis (Chinese gooseberry) and small plums were tested, and only the kiwi showed little change. The apricots may need only 8–10 hours, while the rest were perfect after 24 hours. It's really well worth the test.

MEUSLI BREAKFAST

Meusli is a healthful breakfast invention of the Bircher Benner Institute in Zurich, Switzerland. We have taken the liberty to reduce its calories and fats and simplify the procedure by removing the ground nuts, reducing the honey by half and increasing the volume with low-fat plain yogurt and adding wheat germ and 100% bran cereal for roughage.

4 tbsp. uncooked rolled oats
4 tbsp. lemon juice
4 tbsp. raisins
2 tbsp. liquid honey
4 tbsp. wheat germ

4 tbsp. 100% bran cereal
3 large green apples
  (Granny Smith)
8 oz. yogurt to mix in
8 oz. yogurt to serve on the side

PREPARATION

Soak uncooked oats with raisins in water overnight. Throw out the soaking water.

Combine all ingredients but grate the apples—skin, core and all but the seeds—and add these at the last moment before serving.

Serve well chilled for breakfast with a 5-oz. glass of orange juice and a slice of whole-wheat toast with butter and No-Cook Peach Jam (see page 243). A cup of tea with milk will bring the total up to 331 calories.

NUTRITION PROFILE

	CALO-RIES	PRO-TEIN	SATU-RATED FAT	CARBO-HYDRATE	CAL-CIUM	VITA-MIN A	VITA-MIN C
4 tbsp. oats	32.5	1 gm.		6 gm.	5 mg.		
4 tbsp. lemon juice	20	1 gm.		6 gm.	19 mg.	10 i.u.	39 mg.
4 tbsp. raisins	106.4			29 gm.	24 mg.		
2 tbsp. honey	130			34 gm.	2 mg.		
4 tbsp. wheat germ	98	7 gm.	2.5 gm.	12.4 gm.	12 mg.	25 i.u.	2.5 mg.
4 tbsp. bran	80	4 gm.	1 gm.	25 gm.	27 mg.		
3 apples	210			54 gm.	24 mg.	150 i.u.	15 mg.
16 oz. yogurt	250	16 gm.	4 gm.	26 gm.	588 mg.	340 i.u.	4 mg.
	926.9						

Not counting the yogurt, our Muesli serves 4 at 169.2 calories per serving or 6 at 112.8 calories. Traditional Bircher Muesli has 220 calories per serving.

SPICED PEACHES

A splendid accompaniment to rich meat dishes, such as pork, spareribs, roast beef or lamb, is the spiced fruit garnish. Here we have Spiced Peaches. You can start out with fresh peaches in season, or make up limited quantities as required using preserved fruit.

1 lb. (drained wt.) water-packed
sliced peaches or peach halves

Reserved liquid from peaches
1¼ c. rice vinegar
½ tsp. cloves

1 small cinnamon stick
piece (½ x ¼ in.)
½ tsp. allspice berries

PREPARATION

Simmer last 4 ingredients together for 30 minutes in a covered small saucepan. Strain and pour hot over peaches. Soak for 10 minutes. Pour off the vinegar and re-cover peaches with the original juice from the can.

Index